ESL Grades 2

Contents

Introduction

The *ESL Standards for Pre-K–12 Students* notes that "what is most important for ESOL learners is to function effectively in English and through English while learning challenging academic content." (p. 6) The Steck-Vaughn *ESL* series was designed to meet the needs of both second-language learners and teachers in achieving this goal.

To help ESOL students, the lessons in *ESL*:
• introduce concepts in context.
• highlight specific words or concepts with bold print and rebus clues.
• reinforce the skill with practice.

To help the teacher, the lessons in *ESL*:
• target grade-appropriate concepts.
• offer step-by-step instruction on a beginning, intermediate, and advanced level.
• build background knowledge.
• suggest ideas or words to be shared in the student's native language.
• signal when a phonics skill is unfamiliar to speakers of a specific language.
• point out idioms and multiple-meaning words that could cause confusion.
• suggest extension activities that apply the skill in a real-world situation.

THE ESOL STUDENT

Like all students, second-language learners bring to the classroom a wide variety of experiences, history, and culture. It is important to help these students feel appreciated and respected in the classroom. They have a wealth of knowledge that is interesting and beneficial to all students. By asking them to share stories and experiences about their native country as well as expressions and words in their native language, you will help them feel productive and successful.

 The multicultural icon in the lessons indicates ways for students to share aspects of their language and culture with the class.

ESOL students have different proficiency levels of the English language. Three levels are generally recognized.

Beginning: Students at this level have little or no understanding of the English language. They respond to questions and commands nonverbally by pointing or drawing. Some students at this level may give single word responses. They depend on nonprint clues to decode information in texts. To facilitate learning for beginning language learners, ask questions to which students can gesture to answer or respond with a "yes" or "no." Instruction should be slow, directed, and repetitive.

Intermediate: Intermediate ESOL students have a fundamental grasp of English. They understand and can use basic vocabulary associated with routine situations and needs. These students can respond using simple sentences, but their grammar is inconsistent. To read text, these language learners must have prior knowledge of the concepts. To facilitate learning for intermediate language learners, ask questions to which students can reply with words or short phrases. Instruction should be directed at first to make sure students understand the directions, and the page should be read to insure they know the content. It is also helpful to pair students.

Advanced: Students at this level are able to understand and communicate using English in most routine situations. They may need explanations of idioms, multiple-meaning words, and abstract concepts. They are often fluent readers and writers of English. Instruction for these learners includes responding to higher-level questions, reading the directions, and explaining words and phrases that might be confusing.

ORGANIZATION OF ESL

The *ESL* book is divided into four units.

Readiness: This section reinforces the basic skills students will need in the classroom and many real-world situations. There are two parts to each lesson. Part A introduces the skill or concept with picture clues and bold print to help second-language learners focus on the important words. Part B offers practice in a real-life application.

Phonics: This unit introduces grade-appropriate phonics skills. Each lesson has three sections. Part A introduces the skill or concept with picture clues and bold print words. Part B reinforces the words and the sounds from part A. In part C, students apply the skill. The phonics lessons also identify sounds that some language learners may be unfamiliar with.

 The whirling letter icon indicates multiple-meaning words that may confuse students.

Language Arts: Like the phonics unit, this unit focuses on skills that are grade-appropriate. It also offers instruction in three parts: introduction, reinforcement, and application.

Vocabulary: The vocabulary unit highlights basic words and background knowledge students need to function on a daily level or to understand topics taught in other curriculum areas. Like the readiness unit, two-part lessons first introduce the concept and then give practice applying it.

SPECIAL FEATURES

Individual Student Chart: The Individual Student Chart found on page 3 can help you track each student's skill understanding and progress.

Lessons: Each lesson in Units 2, 3, and 4 is a two-page spread. The left page is the model for teaching the pupil activity sheet, found on the right page. The teacher model explains how to focus on the skill or ways to build background knowledge. Most importantly, the teacher model suggests the steps for teaching the page at each proficiency level.

Certificates: The two certificates on page 122 can be copied and distributed to students. One recognizes the student's efforts, and the other commends the student for successfully attaining a skill.

Take-Home Book: Beginning on page 123, you will find a take-home book about important American symbols. Copies can be distributed to students. You may wish to read aloud the booklet several times before sending it home with students.

Individual Student Chart

Name _____

Skill	Accomplished (yes/no)	Date Page Completed
Unit 1: Readiness		
Circles and Lines		
Top, Middle, and Bottom		
Left and Right		
Above and Below		
In, On, Beside, and Under		
Same		
Different		
Groups		
First, Next, and Last		
Numbers to 10		
Number Words		
Numbers to 20		
ABC Order		
Partner Letters		
Letters and Sounds		
More Letters and Sounds		
A Name		
An Address		
A Telephone Number		
Directions		
More Directions		
Unit 2: Phonics		
Short *a*		
Short *e*		
Short *i*		
Short *o*		
Short *u*		
Long *a* (*a_e*)		
Long *a* (*ay* and *ai*)		
Long *e* (*ee* and *ea*)		
Long *i* (*i_e*)		
Long *o* (*o_e*)		
Long *o* (*oa*)		
Long *u* (*u_e*)		
y as a Vowel		
r-Controlled Vowel *ar*		

Skill	Accomplished (yes/no)	Date Page Completed
r-Controlled Vowel *or*		
r-Controlled Vowels *er, ir, ur*		
s-Blends		
r-Blends		
l-Blends		
Sounds of *c*		
Sounds of *g*		
Sounds of *s*		
Digraphs *ch* and *wh*		
Digraphs *sh* and *th*		
Unit 3: Language Arts		
Naming Words		
Special Names		
More Than One		
Action Words		
Adding *ed*		
Is or *Are*		
Pronouns		
Describing Words		
Compound Words		
Contractions		
Prefixes		
Suffixes		
Unit 4: Vocabulary		
Body Parts		
Clothing		
Colors		
Places in a Community		
Days of the Week		
Food		
Money		
School Tools		
Shapes		
Signs		
Ways to Move		
Weather		

Sample Readiness Lesson

The following lesson can be used as a model for teaching the activity pages in the Readiness unit.

PREPARATION

Preview Part A on the activity page. Duplicate the picture/item shown, either by drawing the item on the board, displaying a magazine picture, or better yet, showing the actual item. Students will need to become familiar with these items before learning concepts. Moreover, it is very important that they actively participate in the learning by moving something or by pantomiming. It will help them better understand the vocabulary and concept.

INTRODUCTION

Display the item and say a short, simple sentence about the concept as it relates to the item. Have students repeat the sentence. Introduce all the vocabulary and encourage students to actively participate as they repeat the words. Write the words on the board.

Beginning

Part A: Distribute the page. Direct students to look at the picture. Read the words or sentence aloud and have students repeat the words as they point to the picture. Ask questions about the picture to which students can respond with a nonverbal response or a yes/no answer.

Part B: Explain what students will do in Part B. Have them point to the first picture or word. Identify the picture name or word for students to repeat. Direct students through each step to find and write the answer. Again, if possible, have students actively participate in the process. Repeat with each picture or word.

Intermediate

Part A: Distribute the page. Direct students to look at the picture. Read the words or sentence aloud and have students repeat. Ask questions about the picture to which students can choose one of two answers or the answer can be found in a visual clue.

Part B: Explain what students will do in Part B. Have them point to the first picture or word. Identify the picture name or word for students to repeat. Ask questions that help students find and write the answer. After modeling how to do the work, read each remaining problem, but pause for students to find and write the answer on their own.

Advanced

Part A: Distribute the page. Direct students to look at the picture. Read the words or sentence aloud and have students repeat. Invite students to talk about the picture. Encourage vocabulary development and practice as students talk.

Part B: Read the directions aloud. Ask students to skim the page to see if they have a question about any of the words or pictures. Have students complete the page independently.

Name _____   Date _____

Circles and Lines

A.

_____

circle   **line**

B. Put your pencil on each dot. Follow the arrow. Trace the circles and lines.

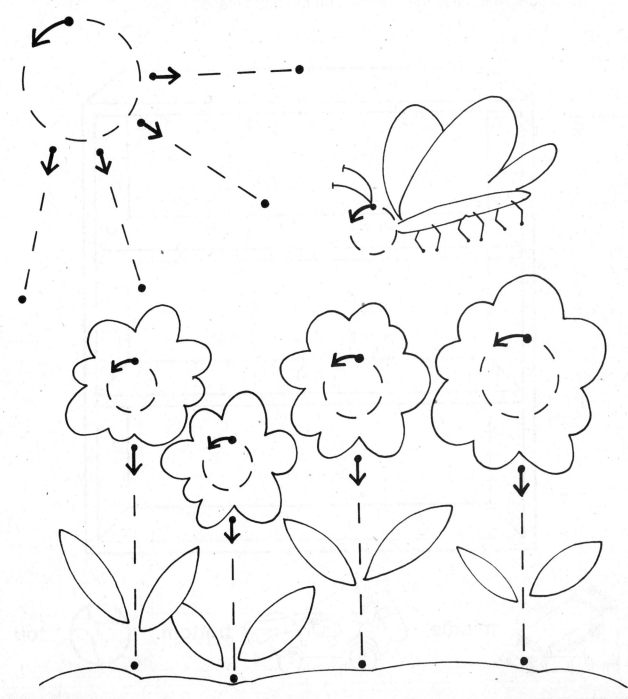

Top, Middle, and Bottom

A.  top
middle
bottom

B. Cut out the pictures and words. Glue the ⚾ on the top shelf. Glue the 📚 on the middle shelf. Glue the 🚗 on the bottom shelf.

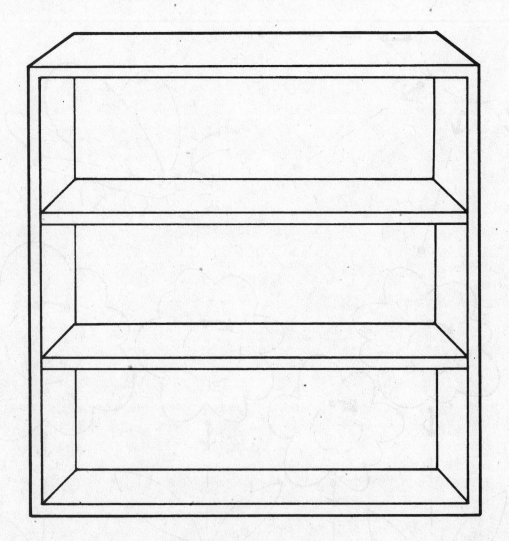

 **middle**    **bottom**   **top**

Left and Right

A.

B. Write **left** or **right** on the lines. Cut out the pictures. Glue the 🚗 on the left. Glue

the 🚲 on the right.

_____   _____

Name _____ Date _____

Above and Below

A.

above

below   below

B. Cut out the pictures. Do the pictures show things that belong above or below the ship? Glue them in the boxes to show the answer. Write **above** or **below**.

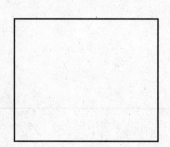

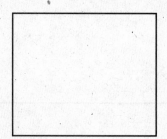

1. _____   2. _____

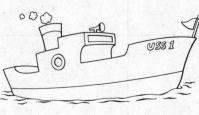

3. _____   4. _____

In, On, Beside, and Under

A.

| in | on | beside | under |

B. Draw a **bird** to show each place.

1. under

2. beside

3. in

4. on

Same

A.

same

B. Make the pictures the same. Draw each missing part.

1.

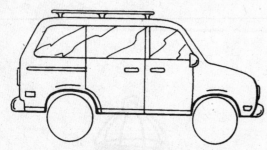 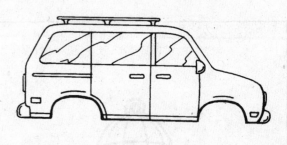

2.

3.

Different

A.

different

B. Which picture is different? Write an **X** on it.

1.

2.

3.

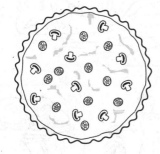  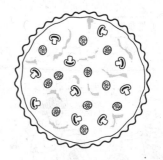

Groups

A.

This is a **group** of balls.

B. Cut out the pictures. Sort the pictures into 2 groups. Tell about your groups.

First, Next, and Last

A.

first   **next**   **last**

B. Tell the order. Write **first**, **next**, and **last**.

1.

_____   _____   _____

2.

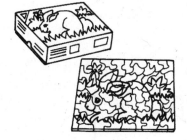  

_____   _____   _____

3.

_____   _____   _____

Numbers to 10

A. 1 2 3 4 5 6 7 8 9 10

B. Connect the dots in order.

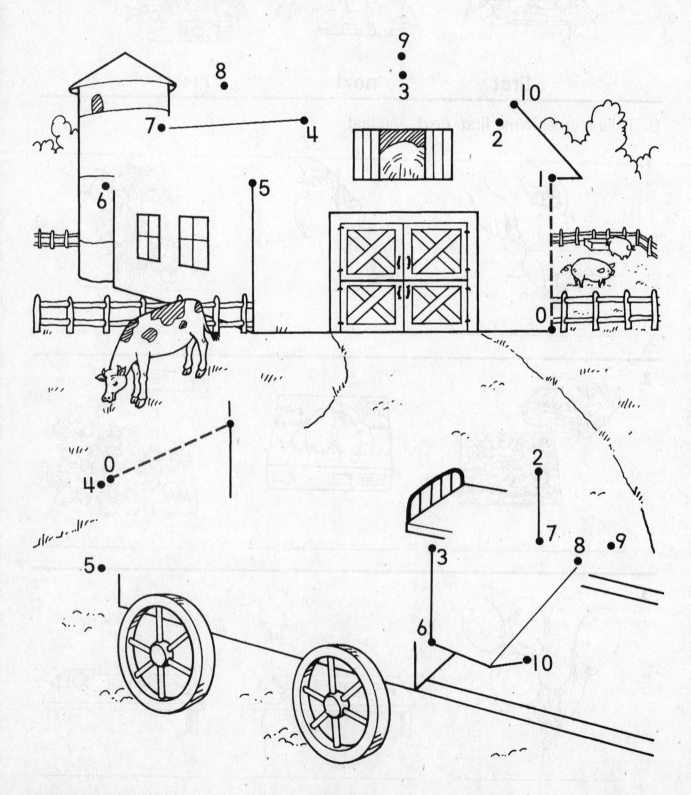

Number Words

A.

1	2	3	4	5	6	7	8	9	10
one	two	three	four	five	six	seven	eight	nine	ten

B. Write the word name for the number.

Numbers to 20

A.

1	2	3	4	5	6	7	8	9	10
11	12	13	14	15	16	17	18	19	20

B. Draw lines to the numbers in order.

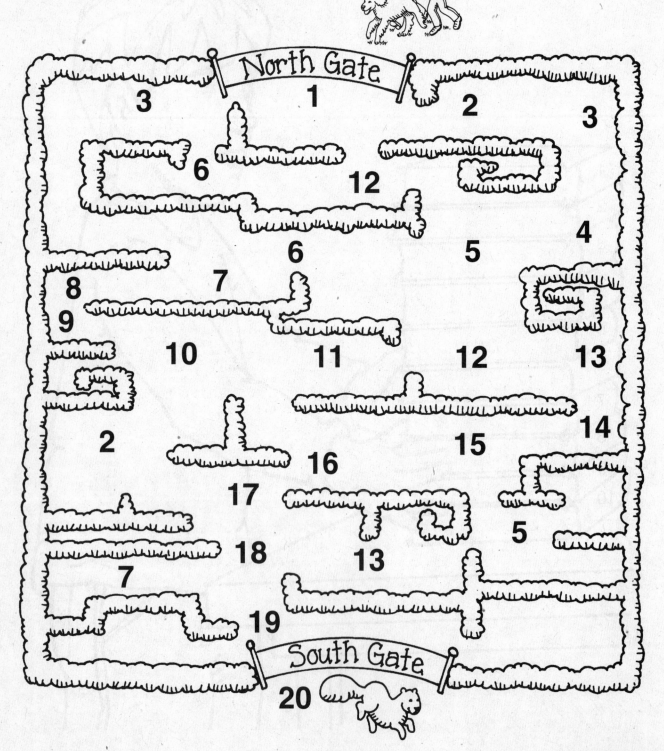

Unit 1: Readiness

ESL 2-3, SV 7097-1

ABC Order

A. Aa Bb Cc Dd Ee Ff Gg Hh Ii Jj Kk Ll Mm
Nn Oo Pp Qq Rr Ss Tt Uu Vv Ww Xx Yy Zz

B. Connect the dots in ABC order.

1.
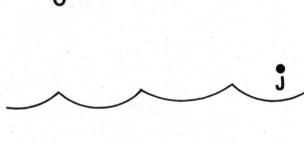
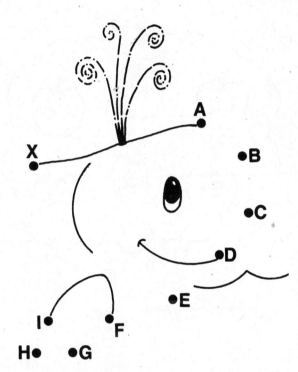

2.
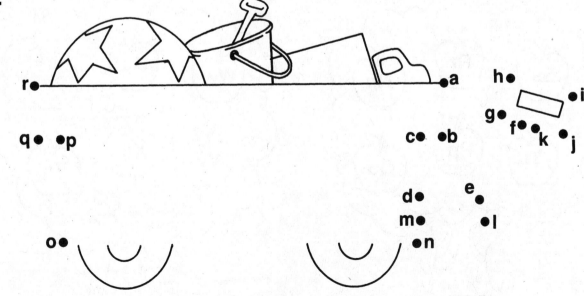

www.svschoolsupply.com
© Steck-Vaughn Company

Unit 1: Readiness
ESL 2-3, SV 7097-1

Partner Letters

A. Aa Bb Cc Dd Ee Ff Gg Hh Ii Jj Kk Ll Mm

Nn Oo Pp Qq Rr Ss Tt Uu Vv Ww Xx Yy Zz

B. Color the apples to show the letters that match.

1.
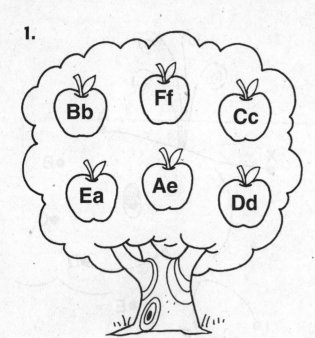

2.

3.

4.

Name _____   Date _____

Letters and Sounds

A.

<u>d</u>og   <u>p</u>an

B. Circle the letter that tells the beginning sound of each picture name.

1.
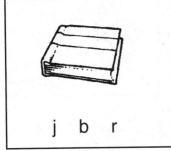

j b r

2.
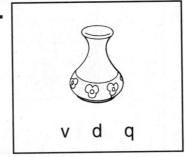

v d q

3.

c k h

4.

f n z

5.

g a l

6.
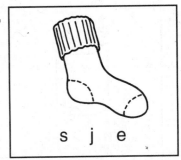

s j e

7.

u p n

8.

t o r

9.
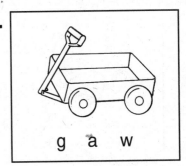

g a w

10.

m q z

11.
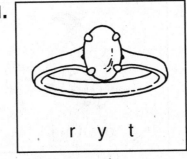

r y t

12.
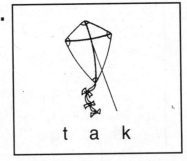

t a k

Unit 1: Readiness
ESL 2-3, SV 7097-1

More Letters and Sounds

A.

__fan__ __wig__

B. Circle the letter that tells the beginning sound of each picture name.

1.

j   o   m

2.

g   b   t

3.
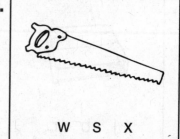

w   s   x

4.

m   c   l

5.
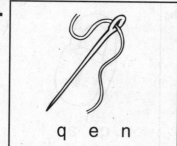

q   e   n

6.

y   z   d

7.

m   f   p

8.

h   d   i

9.
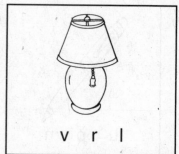

v   r   l

10.

b   a   q

11.

g   t   j

12.
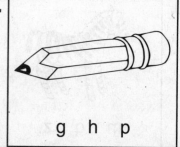

g   h   p

Name _____ Date _____

A Name

A.

My **name** is **Marco Fuentes**.
The **name** of my friend is **Rob Wilson**.

B. Write your name on the T-shirt. Then, color the shirt. Work with friends to complete the sentences.

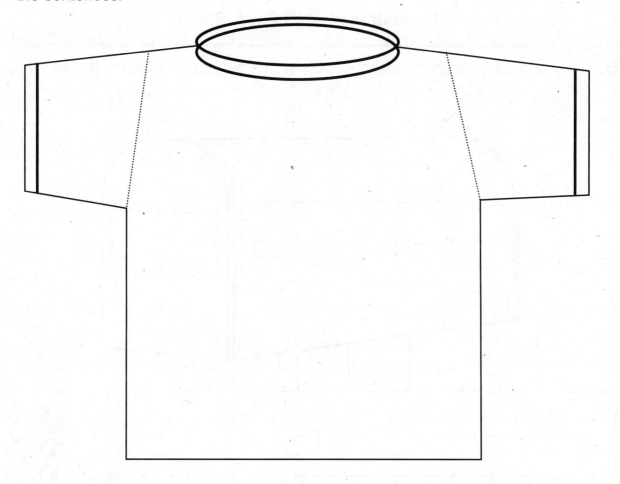

My name is _____.

The name of my friend is _____.

The name of my friend is _____.

The name of my friend is _____.

An Address

A.

Marco Fuentes
123 South Street
Raleigh, North Carolina 27613

Rob Wilson
1243 Maple Street
Portland, Oregon 97219

My **address** is 123 South Street.

B. Write your address on the mailbox. Work with a partner to complete the envelope.

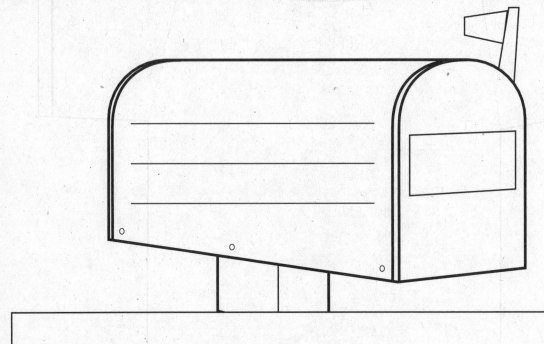

Name _____ Date _____

A Telephone Number

A.

My **telephone number** is 555-2468.
The **telephone number** for Rob is 555-9753.

B. Color the buttons that show your telephone number.
Work with friends to complete the sentences.

My telephone number is _____.

The telephone number for _____ is

_____.

The telephone number for _____ is

_____.

The telephone number for _____ is

_____.

Directions

A.

   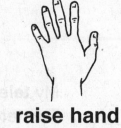 

look   **listen**   **raise hand**   **say**

B. Look at each picture. Write a word from above to tell what the children in the picture are doing.

1.

_____

2.

_____

3.

_____

4.

_____

Name _____   Date _____

More Directions

A.
(circle)   <u>underline</u>   write    color

---

B. Circle the .

Underline the .

Write your name on the  .

Color the .

Short *a*

NOTE: Students whose native language is Italian may have problems with the short *a* sound.

INTRODUCTION

Display a baseball bat. Say: *This is a bat*. Have students repeat the sentence. Then, ask students what you have. Pass the bat to each student and say: *(Name) has a bat*. Encourage students to repeat the sentence each time. Say *bat* again, stressing the middle sound: /b/-/a/-/a/-/t/. Explain that /a/ is the short *a* sound.

 Invite students to share the word *bat* in their native language.

 The homograph *bat* may confuse students. If possible, provide a picture of a flying bat. Explain that *bat* has two meanings. Say simple sentences that provide context clues of the word's use. (*The bat has wings. Mei has a ball and a bat.*) Have students point to the picture of the flying bat or the baseball bat to show an understanding of the way the word is used.

Beginning

Part A: Distribute page 27. Direct students to look at the first picture. Read the sentence aloud and have students repeat it. Invite each student to repeat the sentence individually. Then, ask the following questions about the picture:
• *Who has the bat? Point to it.*
• *What does the cat have? Point to it.*
• *Does the cat have a ball?*
• *Does the cat have a bat?*

Repeat the sentence, stressing the short *a* sound in each word: *The /k/-/a/-/a/-/t/ /h/-/a/-/a/-/z/ a /b/-/a/-/a/-/t/*. Tell students that *cat, bat*, and *has* all have the short *a* sound. Point out that the words *cat* and *bat* are in dark print.

Part B: Tell students they will write words that name pictures. Have students point to the bat and say the picture name. Then have students point to the words in dark print in the sentence above. Ask questions that help students choose and write the word *bat*. Repeat with the picture of the cat.

Part C: Tell students they will write an *a* under the pictures whose names have the short *a* sound. Identify the picture of the hat. Have students repeat the word. Say the picture name again, stressing the short *a* sound: /h/-/a/-/a/-/t/. Tell students that *hat* has the short *a* sound and have them write an *a*. Continue the process with the remaining pictures by identifying which picture names do or do not have the short *a* sound.

Intermediate

Part A: Follow the directions in Part A of the Beginning section, but substitute these questions:
• *Who has the bat?*
• *What does the cat have?*

Part B: Tell students they will write words that name pictures. Then, help students identify the pictures. Have them complete the section with a partner.

Part C: Tell students they will write an *a* under the pictures whose names have the short *a* sound. Identify the picture of the hat. Have students repeat the word. Say the picture name again, stressing the short *a* sound: /h/-/a/-/a/-/t/. Tell students that *hat* has the short *a* sound and have them write an *a*. Help students identify the names of the remaining pictures. Ask students to work with a partner to complete the page.

Advanced

Part A: Distribute page 27. Direct students to look at the first picture. Read the sentence aloud and have students repeat it. Invite students to talk about the picture. Repeat the sentence, stressing the short *a* sound in each word: *The /k/-/a/-/a/-/t/ /h/-/a/-/a/-/z/ a /b/-/a/-/a/-/t/*. Tell students that *cat, bat*, and *has* all have the short *a* sound. Point out that the words *cat* and *bat* are in dark print.

Parts B and C: Read aloud the directions and identify the pictures. Have students complete the page independently.

EXTENSION

Have students sit in a circle. Pass the bat to individual students and challenge them to name words that have the short *a* sound.

Short *a*

A. Read the sentence.

The **cat** has · a **bat**.

B. Write the name of each picture. Use the words in dark print above.

1.

_____

2.

_____

C. Say each picture name. Write the letter **a** under the picture if you hear the short *a* sound.

3.

_____

4.

_____

5.

_____

6.

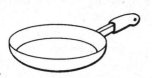

_____

7.

_____

8.

_____

Short e

NOTE: Students whose native language is Urdu may have problems with the short e sound.

INTRODUCTION

Display a picture of a hen. Say: *This is a hen.* Have students repeat the sentence. Then, ask students what sound a hen makes. Tell students that you will say a list of words. Ask them to make the sound of a hen when they hear the word *hen*. Then, slowly say: *cow, hen, cat, hen, goat, dog, hen.* Display the picture again and say *hen*, stressing the middle sound: */h/-/e/-/e/-/n/.* Explain that /e/ is the short e sound.

 The sound a hen makes may be different in other languages. Point out the sounds as students name them. Read the word list above several times, choosing a different hen sound for students to make.

Beginning

Part A: Distribute page 29. Direct students to look at the first picture. Read the sentence aloud and have students repeat it. Invite each student to repeat the sentence individually. Then, ask the following questions about the picture:
• *Who is in bed? Point to it.*
• *Where is the hen? Point to it.*
• *Is the hen in a boat?*
• *Is the hen in a bed?*

Repeat the sentence, stressing the short e sound in each word: *The /h/-/e/-/e/-/n/ is in /b/-/e/-/e/-/d/.* Tell students that *hen* and *bed* have the short e sound. Point out that the words *hen* and *bed* are in dark print.

Part B: Tell students they will write words that name pictures. Have students point to the bed and say the picture name. Then have students point to the words in dark print in the sentence above. Ask questions that help students choose and write the word *bed*. Repeat with the picture of the hen.

Part C: Tell students they will write words for pictures whose names have the short e sound. Identify the picture of the bell. Have students repeat the word. Say the picture name again, stressing the short e sound: */b/-/e/-/e/-/l/.* Tell students that *bell* is spelled *b, e, l, l.* Help them find the word in the list, write it on the line, and cross out the word once it is chosen. Continue the process with the remaining pictures by identifying the picture and the spelling of the name.

Intermediate

Part A: Follow the directions in Part A of the Beginning section, but substitute these questions:
• *Who is in bed?*
• *Where is the hen?*

Part B: Tell students they will write words that name pictures. Then, help students identify the pictures. Have them complete the section with a partner.

Part C: Tell students they will write words for pictures whose names have the short e sound. Have students point to each word in the box as you read them aloud. Ask students to repeat the words after you. Then, identify the picture of the bell. Help students find and write the word *bell*. Say the picture name again, stressing the short e sound: */b/-/e/-/e/-/l/.* Help students identify the names of the remaining pictures. Ask students to work with a partner to complete the page.

Advanced

Part A: Distribute page 29. Direct students to look at the first picture. Read the sentence aloud and have students repeat it. Invite students to talk about the picture. Repeat the sentence, stressing the short e sound in each word: *The /h/-/e/-/e/-/n/ is in /b/-/e/-/e/-/d/.* Tell students that *hen* and *bed* have the short e sound. Point out that the words *hen* and *bed* are in dark print.

Parts B and C: Read aloud the directions and identify the words in the box and the pictures. Have students complete the page independently.

EXTENSION

Have students draw a picture of a hen and another item that has the short e sound.

Short *e*

A. Read the sentence.

The **hen** is in **bed**.

B. Write the name of each picture. Use the words in dark print above.

1.
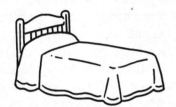

_____

2.

_____

C. Write the word that names the picture.

egg	bell	pen	dress	web	desk

3.

_____

4.

_____

5.

_____

6.

_____

7.

_____

8.

_____

Short *i*

NOTE: Students whose native language is Greek, Italian, or Japanese may have problems with the short *i* sound.

INTRODUCTION

Draw an outline of a pig on the board. Say: *This is a pig.* Have students repeat the sentence. Then, tell students that you are going to tell a story about three pigs. Ask them to raise their hand each time they hear the word *pig.* Then, slowly tell the story of *The Three Little Pigs,* acting out some of the actions of the more difficult words. After the story, say *pig* again, stressing the middle sound: */p/-/i/-/i/-/g/.* Explain that /i/ is the short *i* sound.

 Invite students to share the word *pig* in their native language.

Beginning

Part A: Distribute page 31. Direct students to look at the first picture. Read the sentence aloud and have students repeat it. Invite each student to repeat the sentence individually. Then, ask the following questions about the picture:
• *Who is wearing a wig? Point to it.*
• *What is the pig wearing? Point to it.*
• *Is a pig real?*
• *Does a pig wear a wig?*

Repeat the sentence, stressing the short *i* sound in each word: *The /p/-/i/-/i/-/g/ wears a /w/-/i/-/i/-/g/.* Tell students that *pig* and *wig* have the short *i* sound. Point out that the words *pig* and *wig* are in dark print.

Part B: Tell students they will write words that name pictures. Have students point to the pig and say the picture name. Then, have students point to the words in dark print in the sentence above. Ask questions that help students choose and write the word *pig.* Repeat with the picture of the wig.

Part C: Tell students they will circle words for pictures whose names have the short *i* sound. Identify the picture of the pin. Have students repeat the word. Say the picture name again, stressing the

short *i* sound: */p/-/i/-/i/-/n/.* Then have students point to each word under the picture as you slowly say the words. Check that students circle the correct word. Continue the process with the remaining pictures.

Intermediate

Part A: Follow the directions in Part A of the Beginning section, but substitute these questions:
• *Who is wearing a wig?*
• *What is the pig wearing?*

Part B: Tell students they will write words that name pictures. Then, help students identify the pictures. Have them complete the section with a partner.

Part C: Tell students they will circle words for pictures whose names have the short *i* sound. Ask volunteers what picture they see. Then, have students point to each word under the picture as you read them aloud. Ask students to repeat the words after you. Check that students circle the correct word. Say the picture name again, stressing the short *i* sound: */p/-/i/-/i/-/n/.* Help students identify the names of the remaining pictures and read the words. Ask students to work with a partner to complete the page.

Advanced

Part A: Distribute page 31. Direct students to look at the first picture. Read the sentence aloud and have students repeat it. Invite students to talk about the picture. Repeat the sentence, stressing the short *i* sound in each word: *The /p/-/i/-/i/-/g/ wears a /w/-/i/-/i/-/g/.* Tell students that *pig* and *wig* have the short *i* sound. Point out that the words *pig* and *wig* are in dark print.

Parts B and C: Read aloud the directions and identify the pictures and words. Have students complete the page independently.

EXTENSION

Invite students to act out the story of *The Three Little Pigs* as you retell it.

Short *i*

A. Read the sentence.

The **pig** wears a **wig**.

B. Write the name of each picture. Use the words in dark print above.

1.

_____

2.

_____

C. Circle the word that names the picture.

3.

pan   pin

4.

fish   fun

5.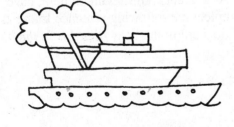

sat   ship

6.

bib   bat

Short o

INTRODUCTION

Display a large empty box. Stand inside the box and say: *(Teacher's name) stands in a box.* Have students repeat the sentence. Then, invite each student to stand in the box and say: *(Name) stands in the box.* Encourage students to repeat the sentence each time. Say *box* again, stressing the middle sound: /b/-/o/-/o/-/x/. Explain that /o/ is the short *o* sound.

 Invite students to share the word *box* in their native language.

 The homograph *box* may confuse students. Explain that *box* has two meanings. Pantomime the sport of boxing and then display the cardboard box. Say simple sentences using the word in both ways and encourage students to pantomime the action or point to the box to show the way the word is used.

Beginning

Part A: Distribute page 33. Direct students to look at the first picture. Read the sentence aloud and have students repeat it. Invite each student to repeat the sentence individually. Then, ask the following questions about the picture:
• *Who is in the box? Point to it.*
• *Where is the fox? Point to it.*
• *Is the fox sitting?*
• *Is the fox in the box?*

Repeat the sentence, stressing the short *o* sound in each word: *A /f/-/o/-/o/-/x/ sits in a /b/-/o/-/o/-/x/.* Tell students that *fox* and *box* both have the short *o* sound. Point out that the words *fox* and *box* are in dark print.

Part B: Tell students they will write words that name pictures. Have students point to the fox and say the picture name. Then, have students point to the words in dark print in the sentence above. Ask questions that help students choose and write the word *fox.* Repeat with the picture of the box.

Part C: Tell students they will write an *o* under the pictures whose names have the short *o* sound. Identify the picture of the mop. Have students repeat the word. Say the picture name again,

stressing the short *o* sound: /m/-/o/-/o/-/p/. Tell students that *mop* has the short *o* sound and have them write an *o.* Continue the process with the remaining pictures by identifying which picture names do or do not have the short *o* sound.

Intermediate

Part A: Follow the directions in Part A of the Beginning section, but substitute these questions:
• *Who is in the box?*
• *Where is the fox?*

Part B: Tell students they will write words that name pictures. Then, help students identify the pictures. Have them complete the section with a partner.

Part C: Tell students they will write an *o* under the pictures whose names have the short *o* sound. Identify the picture of the mop. Have students repeat the word. Say the picture name again, stressing the short *o* sound: /m/-/o/-/o/-/p/. Tell students that *mop* has the short *o* sound and have them write an *o.* Help students identify the names of the remaining pictures. Ask students to work with a partner to complete the page.

Advanced

Part A: Distribute page 33. Direct students to look at the first picture. Read the sentence aloud and have students repeat it. Invite students to talk about the picture. Repeat the sentence, stressing the short *o* sound in each word: *A /f/-/o/-/o/-/x/ sits in a /b/-/o/-/o/-/x/.* Tell students that *fox* and *box* both have the short *o* sound. Point out that the words *fox* and *box* are in dark print.

Parts B and C: Read aloud the directions and identify the pictures. Have students complete the page independently.

EXTENSION

Challenge students to search in the classroom to find items that have the short *o* sound to place in the box. As students return with an item, have them complete the following sentence frame as they put the item in the box: *[Item] is in the box.*

Short o

A. Read the sentence.

A **fox** sits in a **box**.

B. Write the name of each picture. Use the words in dark print above.

1.

_____

2.

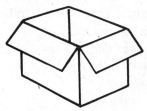

_____

C. Say each picture name. Write **o** under the picture if you hear the short *o* sound.

3.

_____

4.

_____

5.

_____

6.

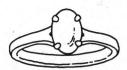

_____

7.

_____

8.

_____

Short *u*

INTRODUCTION

Gather students on a rug. Say: *I can jump on the rug.* Have each student repeat the sentence as they jump. Tell students that you will say a list of words. Ask them to jump when they hear the word *rug.* Then, slowly say: *rug, cat, rug, goat, rug, horse, rug.* Point to the rug and say *rug,* stressing the middle sound: /r/-/u/-/u/-/g/. Explain that /u/ is the short *u* sound.

 Invite students to say the word *rug* in their native language and ask them to tell where they might see a rug in a home.

Beginning

Part A: Distribute page 35. Direct students to look at the first picture. Read the sentence aloud and have students repeat it. Invite partners to pantomime the movement in the picture as they repeat the sentence. Then, ask the following questions about the picture:
• *What are the bugs dancing on? Point to it.*
• *Who do you see on the rug? Point to them.*
• *Are the bugs jumping?*
• *Are the bugs dancing?*

Repeat the sentence, stressing the short *u* sound in each word: *Two /b/-/u/-/u/-/g/-/z/ dance on a /r/-/u/-/u/-/g/.* Tell students that *bugs* and *rug* have the short *u* sound. Point out that the words *bugs* and *rug* are in dark print.

Part B: Tell students they will write words that name pictures. Have students point to the rug and say the picture name. Then, have students point to the words in dark print in the sentence above. Ask questions that help students choose and write the word *rug.* Repeat with the picture of the bugs.

Part C: Tell students they will write words for pictures whose names have the short *u* sound. Identify the picture of the tub. Have students repeat the word. Say the picture name again, stressing the short *u* sound: /t/-/u/-/u/-/b/. Tell students that *tub* is spelled *t, u, b.* Help them find the word in the

list, write it on the line, and cross out the word once it is chosen. Continue the process with the remaining pictures by identifying the picture and the spelling of the name.

Intermediate

Part A: Follow the directions in Part A of the Beginning section, but substitute these questions:
• *Who do you see on the rug?*
• *What are the bugs dancing on?*

Part B: Tell students they will write words that name pictures. Then, help students identify the pictures. Have them complete the section with a partner.

Part C: Tell students they will write words for pictures whose names have the short *u* sound. Have students point to each word in the box as you read them aloud. Ask students to repeat the word after you. Then, identify the picture of the tub. Help students find and write the word *tub.* Say the picture name again, stressing the short *u* sound: /t/-/u/-/u/-/b/. Help students identify the names of the remaining pictures. Ask students to work with a partner to complete the page.

Advanced

Part A: Distribute page 35. Direct students to look at the first picture. Read the sentence aloud and have students repeat it. Invite students to talk about the picture. Repeat the sentence, stressing the short *u* sound in each word: *Two /b/-/u/-/u/-/g/-/z/ dance on a /r/-/u/-/u/-/g/.* Tell students that *bugs* and *rug* have the short *u* sound. Point out that the words *bugs* and *rug* are in dark print.

Parts B and C: Read aloud the directions and the words in the box. Then, identify the pictures. Have students complete the page independently.

EXTENSION

Invite students to draw a picture of bugs jumping on a rug. Help them label the picture.

Name _____ Date _____

Short *u*

A. Read the sentence.

Two **bugs** dance on a **rug**.

B. Write the name of each picture. Use the words in dark print above.

1.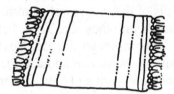

_____

2.

_____

C. Write the word that names the picture.

| drum | brush | truck | duck | bus | tub |

3.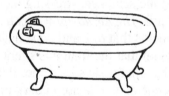

_____

4.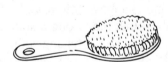

_____

5.

_____

6.

_____

7.

_____

8.

_____

Long a (a_e)

NOTE: Students whose native language is French, Urdu, or Vietnamese may have problems with the long *a* sound.

INTRODUCTION

Make a cape by accordion-pleating one long edge of butcher paper and stapling a paper band on it for a tie. Say: *This is a cape.* Have students repeat the sentence. Show students how a cape is worn and discuss its use. Then, invite each student to wear the cape and say: *(Name) wears a cape.* Encourage students to repeat the sentence each time. Say *cape* again, stressing the middle sound: /k/-/ā/-/ā/-/p/. Explain that /ā/ is the long *a* sound.

 As students begin to complete Part C, point out that *pane* is a homonym of *pain*. Explain the differences in the words to students.

Beginning

Part A: Distribute page 37. Direct students to look at the first picture. Read the sentence aloud and have students repeat it. Invite each student to repeat the sentence individually. Then, ask the following questions about the picture:
• *Who is wearing a cape? Point to it.*
• *What is the ape wearing? Point to it.*
• *Can an ape do tricks?*
• *Does the cape have stars on it?*

Repeat the sentence, stressing the long *a* sound in each word: *The /ā/-/ā/-/p/ wears a /k/-/ā/-/ā/-/p/.* Tell students that *ape* and *cape* have the long *a* sound. Explain that the final *e* is silent and changes the vowel so that it says its name. Point out that the words *ape* and *cape* are in dark print.

Part B: Tell students they will write words that name pictures. Have students point to the cape and say the picture name. Then, have students point to the words in dark print in the sentence above. Ask questions that help students choose and write the word *cape*. Repeat with the picture of the ape.

Part C: Tell students that they will build new words that have the long *a* sound. Then, they will match a picture to the new word they made. Remind students of the *a_e* vowel pattern. Then, identify the picture of the can. Help students write the word *can* and add the final silent *e*. Say the new word and have students repeat it. Guide them to cut out and glue the picture of the cane above

the new word. Continue the process with the words and remaining pictures.

Intermediate

Part A: Follow the directions in Part A of the Beginning section, but substitute these questions:
• *Who is wearing a cape?*
• *What is the ape wearing?*

Part B: Tell students they will write words that name pictures. Then, help students identify the pictures. Have them complete the section with a partner.

Part C: Tell students that they will build new words that have the long *a* sound. Then, they will match a picture to the new word they made. Remind students of the *a_e* vowel pattern. Ask volunteers what picture they see. Then, help students read the word under the can. Next, direct students to write the word *can* and add the final silent *e*. Say the new word and have students repeat it. Guide them to cut out and glue the picture of the cane above the new word. Help students identify the names of the remaining pictures and read the words. Ask students to work with a partner to complete the page.

Advanced

Part A: Distribute page 37. Direct students to look at the first picture. Read the sentence aloud and have students repeat it. Invite students to talk about the picture. Repeat the sentence, stressing the long *a* sound in each word: *The /ā/-/ā/-/p/ wears a /k/-/ā/-/ā/-/p/.* Tell students that *ape* and *cape* have the long *a* sound. Explain that the final *e* is silent and changes the vowel so that it says its name. Point out that the words *ape* and *cape* are in dark print.

Parts B and C: Read aloud the directions and identify the pictures and words. Have students complete the page independently.

EXTENSION

Tell students that the ape in the picture also likes to play games. Point out that *game* follows the *a_e* pattern. Allow students to play games.

Name _____   Date _____

Long *a* (*a_e*)

A. Read the sentence.

This **ape** wears a **cape**.

B. Write the name of each picture. Use the words in dark print above.

1.

_____

2.

_____

C. Rewrite each word and add an **e** to the end. Then, cut out the pictures. Glue the picture to show the meaning of the new word.

3.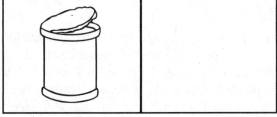

can _____

4.

pan _____

5.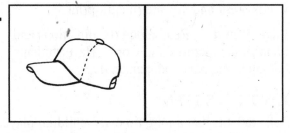

cap _____

6.

tap _____

  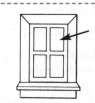 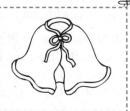

Long *a* (*ay* and *ai*)

NOTE: Students whose native language is French, Urdu, or Vietnamese may have problems with the long *a* sound.

INTRODUCTION

Provide a handful of hay. Say: *This is hay.* Have students repeat the sentence. Say *hay* again, stressing the long *a* sound: /h/-/ā/-/ā/. Remind students that /ā/ is the long *a* sound. Explain that the long *a* sound has several spelling patterns. Write *hay*, *rain*, and *cape* on the board and underline the long *a* spelling pattern in each. Say the words as you point to them and have students repeat the words. Discuss the differences in the spelling patterns. Tell students that they will learn words that have the *ai* and *ay* patterns.

 Invite students to say the word *hay* in their native language and tell what kinds of animals eat hay.

 As students work Part C, point out that *pail* is a homonym of *pale*. Explain the differences in the words to students.

Beginning

Part A: Distribute page 39. Direct students to look at the first picture. Read the sentence aloud and have students repeat it. Invite each student to repeat the sentence individually. Then, ask the following questions about the picture:
• *Where is the quail sleeping? Point to it.*
• *Who is sleeping in the hay? Point to it.*
• *Is the cat in the hay?*
• *Is the quail in the hay?*

Repeat the sentence, stressing the long *a* sound in each word: *The /kw/-/ā/-/ā/-/l/ sleeps in the /h/-/ā/-/ā/.* Tell students that *quail* and *hay* have the long *a* sound. Remind students of the different spelling patterns for long *a*. Point out that the words *quail* and *hay* are in dark print.

Part B: Tell students they will write words that name pictures. Have students point to the quail and say the picture name. Then, have students point to the words in dark print in the sentence above. Ask questions that help students choose and write the word *quail*. Repeat with the picture of the hay.

Part C: Tell students they will circle words for pictures whose names have the long *a* sound. Identify the picture of the train. Have students repeat the word. Say the picture name again,

stressing the long *a* sound: /tr/-/ā/-/ā/-/n/. Then, have students point to each word under the picture as you slowly say the words. Check that students circle the correct word. Continue the process with the remaining pictures.

Intermediate

Part A: Follow the directions in Part A of the Beginning section, but substitute these questions:
• *Who is sleeping in the hay?*
• *Where is the quail sleeping?*

Part B: Tell students they will write words that name pictures. Then, help students identify the pictures. Have them complete the section with a partner.

Part C: Tell students they will circle words for pictures whose names have the long *a* sound. Ask volunteers what picture they see. Then, have students point to each word under the picture as you read them aloud. Ask students to repeat the words after you. Check that students circle the correct word. Say the picture name again, stressing the long *a* sound: /tr/-/ā/-/ā/-/n/. Help students identify the names of the remaining pictures and read the words. Ask students to work with a partner to complete the page.

Advanced

Part A: Distribute page 39. Direct students to look at the first picture. Read the sentence aloud and have students repeat it. Invite students to talk about the picture. Repeat the sentence, stressing the long *a* sound in each word: *The /kw/-/ā/-/ā/-/l/ sleeps in the /h/-/ā/-/ā/.* Tell students that *quail* and *hay* have the long *a* sound. Remind students of the different spelling patterns for long *a*. Point out that the words *quail* and *hay* are in dark print.

Parts B and C: Read aloud the directions and identify the pictures and words. Have students complete the page independently.

EXTENSION

Tell students that a long time ago children played a game called *jackstraws*. The game *pick-up sticks* is based on the old game. Explain that the word *hay* is another word for *straw*. Then, drop a handful of hay. Invite students to pick up a piece of hay without moving other pieces.

Long *a* (*ay* and *ai*)

A. Read the sentence.

The **quail** sleeps in the **hay**.

B. Write the name of each picture. Use the words in dark print above.

1.

_____

2.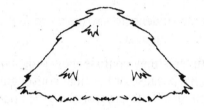

_____

C. Circle the word that names the picture.

3.

train take

4.

jail jay

5.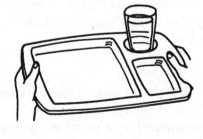

rain tray

6.

pail pay

Long e (ee and ea)

NOTE: Students whose native language is French, Greek, Urdu, or Vietnamese may have problems with the long *e* sound.

INTRODUCTION

Display a leaf. Say: *This is a leaf.* Have students repeat the sentence. Say *leaf* again, stressing the middle sound: /l/-/ē/-/ē/-/f/. Remind students that /ē/ is the long *e* sound. Explain that the long *e* sound has several spelling patterns. Write *leaf* and *bee* on the board and underline the long *e* spelling pattern in each. Say the words as you point to them and have students repeat the words. Discuss the differences in the spelling patterns. Tell students that they will learn words that have the *ee* and *ea* patterns for long *e*.

 Invite students to say the word *leaf* in their native language.

 Students may confuse the words *leaf* and *leave* because of the final consonant sounds. Write the words on the board and pronounce them slowly, stressing the ending sound. Use the words in context and have students point to the word used in each sentence.

Beginning

Part A: Distribute page 41. Direct students to look at the first picture. Read the sentence aloud and have students repeat it. Invite each student to repeat the sentence individually. Then, ask the following questions about the picture:
• *Where is the bee? Point to it.*
• *What is on the leaf? Point to it.*
• *Is the bee on a light?*
• *Is the bee on a leaf?*

Repeat the sentence, stressing the long *e* sound in each word: *The /b/-/ē/-/ē/ is on the /l/-/ē/-/ē/-/f/.* Tell students that *bee* and *leaf* have the long *e* sound. Remind students of the different spelling patterns for long *e*. Point out that the words *bee* and *leaf* are in dark print.

Part B: Tell students they will write words that name pictures. Have students point to the bee and say the picture name. Then, have students point to the words in dark print in the sentence above. Ask questions that help students choose and write the word *bee*. Repeat with the picture of the leaf.

Part C: Tell students they will write words for pictures whose names have the long *e* sound.

Identify the picture of the feet. Have students repeat the word. Say the picture name again, stressing the long *e* sound: /f/-/ē/-/ē/-/t/. Tell students that *feet* is spelled *f, e, e, t*. Help them find the word in the list, write it on the line, and cross out the word once it is chosen. Continue the process with the remaining pictures by identifying the picture and the spelling of the name.

Intermediate

Part A: Follow the directions in Part A of the Beginning section, but substitute these questions:
• *What is on the leaf?*
• *Where is the bee?*

Part B: Tell students they will write words that name pictures. Then, help students identify the pictures. Have them complete the section with a partner.

Part C: Tell students they will write words for pictures whose names have the long *e* sound. Have students point to each word in the box as you read them aloud. Ask students to repeat the word after you. Then, identify the picture of the feet. Help students find and write the word *feet*. Say the picture name again, stressing the long *e* sound: /f/-/ē/-/ē/-/t/. Help students identify the names of the remaining pictures. Ask students to work with a partner to complete the page.

Advanced

Part A: Distribute page 41. Direct students to look at the first picture. Read the sentence aloud and have students repeat it. Invite students to talk about the picture. Repeat the sentence, stressing the long *e* sound in each word: *The /b/-/ē/-/ē/ is on the /l/-/ē/-/ē/-/f/.* Tell students that *bee* and *leaf* have the long *e* sound. Remind students of the different spelling patterns for long *e*. Point out that the words *bee* and *leaf* are in dark print.

Parts B and C: Read aloud the directions and identify the pictures. Have students complete the page independently.

EXTENSION

Gather leaves of different shapes. Invite students to trace them. Then, challenge students to write words that contain the long *e* sound on the leaves.

Long e (ee and ea)

A. Read the sentence.

The **bee** is on the **leaf**.

B. Write the name of each picture. Use the words in dark print above.

1.

_____

2.

_____

C. Write the word that names the picture.

| queen | sheep | peas | feet | meat | eat |

3.
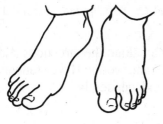

_____

4.
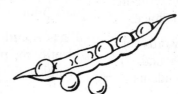

_____

5.

_____

6.
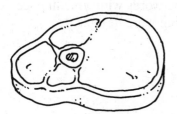

_____

7.

_____

8.

_____

Long *i* (i_e)

INTRODUCTION

Display an ice cube. Say: *This is ice.* Have students repeat the sentence. Invite each student to hold the ice and repeat the sentence again. Say *ice*, stressing the initial sound: /ī/-/ī/-/s/. Explain that /ī/ is the long *i* sound.

 Invite students to share the word *ice* in their native language.

Beginning

Part A: Distribute page 43. Direct students to look at the first picture. Read the sentence aloud and have students repeat it. Briefly discuss the action of ice skating. Invite each student to repeat the sentence individually. Ask the following questions about the picture:
• *Who is skating on the ice? Point to them.*
• *What are the mice skating on? Point to it.*
• *Are dogs skating on ice?*
• *Are mice skating on ice?*

Repeat the sentence, stressing the long *i* sound in each word: *The /m/-/ī/-/ī/-/s/ skate on /ī/-/ī/-/s/.* Tell students that *mice* and *ice* have the long *i* sound. Explain that the final *e* is silent and changes the vowel so that it says its name. Point out that the words *mice* and *ice* are in dark print.

Part B: Tell students they will write words that name pictures. Have students point to the ice and say the picture name. Then, have students point to the words in dark print in the sentence above. Ask questions that help students choose and write the word *ice*. Repeat with the picture of the mice.

Part C: Tell students they will circle words for pictures whose names have the long *i* sound. Identify the picture of the kite. Have students repeat the word. Say the picture name again, stressing the long *i* sound: /k/-/ī/-/ī/-/t/. Then have students point to each word under the picture as you slowly say the words. Check that students circle the correct word. Continue the process with the remaining pictures.

Intermediate

Part A: Follow the directions in Part A of the Beginning section, but substitute these questions:
• *Who is ice skating?*
• *What are the mice skating on?*

Part B: Tell students they will write words that name pictures. Then, help students identify the pictures. Have them complete the section with a partner.

Part C: Tell students they will circle words for pictures whose names have the long *i* sound. Ask volunteers what picture they see. Then, have students point to each word under the picture as you read them aloud. Ask students to repeat the words after you. Check that students circle the correct word. Say the picture name again, stressing the long *i* sound: /k/-/ī/-/ī/-/t/. Help students identify the names of the remaining pictures and read the words. Ask students to work with a partner to complete the page.

Advanced

Part A: Distribute page 43. Direct students to look at the first picture. Read the sentence aloud and have students repeat it. Invite students to talk about the picture. Repeat the sentence, stressing the long *i* sound in each word: *The /m/-/ī/-/ī/-/s/ skate on /ī/-/ī/-/s/.* Tell students that *mice* and *ice* have the long *i* sound. Explain that the final *e* is silent and changes the vowel so that it says its name. Point out that the words *mice* and *ice* are in dark print.

Parts B and C: Read aloud the directions and identify the pictures and words. Have students complete the page independently.

EXTENSION

Provide students with colored chalk and construction paper. Then, invite students to write words that have the spelling pattern *i_e* for long *i*. Have them rub the words with a melting ice cube to create interesting word designs.

Long *i* (*i_e*)

A. Read the sentence.

The **mice** skate on **ice**.

B. Write the name of each picture. Use the words in dark print above.

1.

_____

2.

_____

C. Circle the word that names the picture.

3.

kite   hide

4.

dime   dive

5.

bike   bite

6.

nice   nine

Long o (o_e)

NOTE: Students whose native language is Chinese or Korean may have problems with the long *o* sound.

INTRODUCTION

Display a picture of a rose. Say: *This is a rose.* Have students repeat the sentence. Pass the picture to each student and say: *(Name) is holding a rose.* Encourage the students to repeat the sentence each time. Say *rose* again, stressing the long *o* sound: /r/-/ō/-/z/. Explain that /ō/ is the long *o* sound.

 Invite students to share the word *rose* in their native language.

 The homograph *rose* may confuse students. Explain that *rose* has two meanings and define them. Then, say simple sentences that provide context clues of the word's use. (*A rose is a kind of flower. John rose early in the morning to get ready for school.*) Invite students to clap when they hear a sentence in which *rose* refers to a flower.

Beginning

Part A: Distribute page 45. Direct students to look at the first picture. Read the sentence aloud and have students repeat it. Invite each student to repeat the sentence individually. Then, ask the following questions about the picture:
• *Who smells the rose? Point to it.*
• *What is the mole smelling? Point to it.*
• *Is a mole smelling a rose?*
• *Is a mole smelling a goat?*

Repeat the sentence, stressing the long *o* sound in each word: *The /m/-/ō/-/l/ smells a /r/-/ō/-/z/.* Tell students that *mole* and *rose* have the long *o* sound. Explain that the final *e* is silent and changes the vowel so that it says its name. Point out that the words *mole* and *rose* are in dark print.

Part B: Tell students they will write words that name pictures. Have students point to the rose and say the picture name. Then, have students point to the words in dark print in the sentence above. Ask questions that help students choose and write the word *rose*. Repeat with the picture of the mole.

Part C: Tell students they will write words for pictures whose names have the long *o* sound. Identify the picture of the robe. Have students repeat the word. Say the picture name again, stressing the long *o* sound: /r/-/ō/-/ō/-/b/. Tell

students that *robe* is spelled *r, o, b, e.* Help them find the word in the list, write it on the line, and cross out the word once it is chosen. Continue the process with the remaining pictures by identifying the picture and the spelling of the name.

Intermediate

Part A: Follow the directions in Part A of the Beginning section, but substitute these questions:
• *Who smells the rose?*
• *What is the mole smelling?*

Part B: Tell students they will write words that name pictures. Then, help students identify the pictures. Have them complete the section with a partner.

Part C: Tell students they will write words for pictures whose names have the long *o* sound. Identify the picture of the robe. Have students repeat the word. Say the picture name again, stressing the long *o* sound: /r/-/ō/-/ō/-/b/. Tell students that *robe* is spelled *r, o, b, e.* Help them find the word in the list, write it on the line, and cross out the word once it is chosen. Help students identify the names of the remaining pictures and read the words. Ask students to work with a partner to complete the page.

Advanced

Part A: Distribute page 45. Direct students to look at the first picture. Read the sentence aloud and have students repeat it. Invite students to talk about the picture. Repeat the sentence, stressing the long *o* sound in each word: *The /m/-/ō/-/l/ smells a /r/-/ō/-/ō/-/z/.* Tell students that *mole* and *rose* have the long *o* sound. Explain that the final *e* is silent and changes the vowel so that it says its name. Point out that the words *mole* and *rose* are in dark print.

Parts B and C: Read aloud the directions and identify the pictures and words. Have students complete the page independently.

EXTENSION

Invite students to draw a picture of a rose. Then, spray perfume on the drawing.

Long o (o_e)

A. Read the sentence.

 The **mole** smells a **rose**.

B. Write the name of each picture. Use the words in dark print above.

1.

_____

2.

_____

C. Write the word that names the picture.

| hose | rope | cone | nose | home | robe |

3.

_____

4.

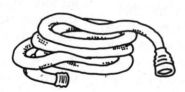

_____

5.

_____

6.

_____

7.

_____

8.

_____

Long o (oa)

NOTE: Students whose native language is Chinese or Korean may have problems with the long *o* sound.

INTRODUCTION

Display a coat. Say: *(Teacher's name) wears a coat.* Have students repeat the sentence. Invite students to put on the coat. Say: *(Name) wears a coat.* Encourage students to repeat the sentence each time. Say *coat* again, stressing the middle sound: /k/-/ō/-/ō/-/t/. Explain that /ō/ is the long *o* sound.

 Invite students to share the word *coat* in their native language.

Beginning

Part A: Distribute page 47. Direct students to look at the first picture. Read the sentence aloud and have students repeat it. Invite each student to repeat the sentence indivdually. Ask the following questions about the picture:
• *Who is wearing the coat? Point to it.*
• *What is the goat wearing? Point to it.*
• *Is a cat wearing the coat?*
• *Is a goat wearing the coat?*

Repeat the sentence, stressing the long *o* sound in each word: *The /g/-/ō/-/ō/-/t/ wears a /k/-/ō/-/ō/-/t/.* Tell students that *goat* and *coat* have the long *o* sound. Remind students of the different spelling patterns for long *o*. Point out that the words *goat* and *coat* are in dark print.

Part B: Tell students they will write words that name pictures. Have students point to the goat and say the picture name. Then, have students point to the words in dark print in the sentence above. Ask questions that help students choose and write the word *goat*. Repeat with the picture of the coat.

Part C: Tell students they will write the letters *oa* on the lines to complete the names for pictures whose names have the long *o* sound. Identify the picture of the road. Have students repeat the word. Say the picture name again, stressing the long *o* sound: /r/-/ō/-/ō/-/d/. Guide students to write the letters as you say them. Check that students write the correct letters. Have students say the word

again. Continue the process with the remaining pictures.

Intermediate

Part A: Follow the directions in Part A of the Beginning section, but substitute these questions:
• *Who is wearing a coat?*
• *What is the goat wearing?*

Part B: Tell students they will write words that name pictures. Then, help students identify the pictures. Have them complete the section with a partner.

Part C: Tell students they will write the letters *oa* on the lines to complete the names for pictures whose names have the long *o* sound. Identify the picture of the road. Have students repeat the word. Say the picture name again, stressing the long *o* sound: /r/-/ō/-/ō/-/d/. Guide students to write the letters as you say them. Check that students write the correct letters. Have students say the word again. Help students identify the names of the remaining pictures. Ask students to work with a partner to complete the page.

Advanced

Part A: Distribute page 47. Direct students to look at the first picture. Read the sentence aloud and have students repeat it. Invite students to talk about the picture. Repeat the sentence, stressing the long *o* sound in each word: *The /g/-/ō/-/ō/-/t/ wears a /k/-/ō/-/ō/-/t/.* Tell students that *goat* and *coat* have the long *o* sound. Remind students of the different spelling patterns for long *o*. Point out that the words *goat* and *coat* are in dark print.

Parts B and C: Read aloud the directions and identify the pictures. Have students complete the page independently.

EXTENSION

Draw a large outline of a coat on butcher paper. Invite students to write words that have the *oa* spelling pattern for long *o* on the coat.

Long o (oa)

A. Read the sentence.

The **goat** wears a **coat**.

B. Write the name of each picture. Use the words in dark print above.

1.

_____

2.

_____

C. Write **oa** to complete the words.

3.

r ___ ___ d

4.

s ___ ___ p

5.

t ___ ___ d

6.

b ___ ___ t

Long *u* (u_e)

NOTE: Students whose native language is Chinese or Korean may have problems with the long *u* sound.

INTRODUCTION

Display a picture of a flute. Say: *This is a flute.* Have students repeat the sentence. Pass the picture to each student and say: *(Name) is holding the flute.* Encourage students to repeat the sentence each time. Say *flute* again, stressing the *u* sound: /fl/-/ū/-/ū/-/t/. Explain that /ū/ is the long *u* sound.

 Invite students to name and describe an instrument in their native country that looks like or is played like a flute.

Beginning

Part A: Distribute page 49. Direct students to look at the first picture. Read the sentence aloud and have students repeat it. Invite each student to repeat the sentence individually. Then, ask the following questions about the picture:
• *Who plays the flute? Point to it.*
• *What is the mule playing? Point to it.*
• *Does the mule have a flute?*
• *Does the mule have glue?*

Repeat the sentence, stressing the long *u* sound in each word: *The /m/-/ū/-/ū/-/l/ plays a /fl/-/ū/-/ū/-/t/.* Tell students that *mule* and *flute* have the long *u* sound. Explain that the final *e* is silent and changes the vowel so that it says its name. Point out that the words *mule* and *flute* are in dark print.

Part B: Tell students they will write words that name pictures. Have students point to the flute and say the picture name. Then, have students point to the words in dark print in the sentence above. Ask questions that help students choose and write the word *flute*. Repeat with the picture of the mule.

Part C: Tell students they will circle words for pictures whose names have the long *u* sound. Identify the picture of the June calendar. Have students repeat the word. Say the picture name again, stressing the long *u* sound: /j/-/ū/-/ū/-/n/. Then have students point to each word under the picture as you slowly say the words. Check that students circle the correct word. Continue the process with the remaining pictures.

Intermediate

Part A: Follow the directions in Part A of the Beginning section, but substitute these questions:
• *Who plays the flute?*
• *What is the mule playing?*

Part B: Tell students they will write words that name pictures. Then, help students identify the pictures. Have them complete the section with a partner.

Part C: Tell students they will circle words for pictures whose names have the long *u* sound. Ask volunteers what picture they see. Then, have students point to the words under the picture as you read them aloud. Ask students to repeat the words after you. Check that students circle the correct word. Say the picture name again, stressing the long *u* sound: /j/-/ū/-/ū/-/n/. Help students identify the names of the remaining pictures and read the words. Ask students to work with a partner to complete the page.

Advanced

Part A: Distribute page 49. Direct students to look at the first picture. Read the sentence aloud and have students repeat it. Invite students to talk about the picture. Repeat the sentence, stressing the long *u* sound in each word: *The /m/-/ū/-/ū/-/l/ plays a /fl/-/ū/-/ū/-/t/.* Tell students that *mule* and *flute* have the long *u* sound. Explain that the final *e* is silent and changes the vowel so that it says its name. Point out that the words *mule* and *flute* are in dark print.

Parts B and C: Read aloud the directions and identify the pictures and words. Have students complete the page independently.

EXTENSION

Tell students that the word *tune* has the long *u* sound. Invite volunteers to share tunes they know from their native country.

Long *u* (*u_e*)

A. Read the sentence.

 The **mule** plays a **flute**.

B. Write the name of each picture. Use the words in dark print above.

1.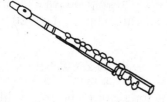

_____

2.

_____

C. Circle the word that names the picture.

3.

June   fuse

4.

cube   tube

5.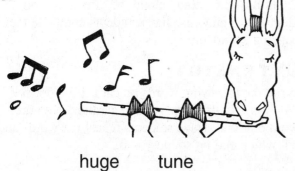

huge   tune

6.

rule   glue

y as a Vowel

NOTE: Students whose native language is French, Greek, Urdu, or Vietnamese may have problems with the long *e* sound.

INTRODUCTION

Draw a picture of a fly with a huge smile on the board. Then write this sentence: *The fly is happy.* Read it out loud and have students repeat it. Invite students to draw their own pictures of flies and to repeat the sentence. Point out that the words *fly* and *happy* both end in the letter *y*. Explain that *y* stands for the long *i* sound in one-syllable words and the long *e* sound in multiple-syllable words.

 Invite students to share the word *fly* in their native language.

 The homograph *fly* may confuse students. Explain that *fly* has two meanings and define them. Then, say simple sentences that provide context clues of the word's use. (*Jan will fly on an airplane. A fly is a bug with wings.*) Invite students to clap when they hear a sentence in which *fly* refers to an insect.

Beginning

Part A: Distribute page 51. Direct students to look at the first picture. Read the sentence aloud and have students repeat it. Then, invite pairs of students to act out the scene and repeat the sentence when they are done. Next, ask the following questions about the picture:
• *What is chasing the fly? Point to it.*
• *What is moving away from the puppy? Point to it.*
• *Is a puppy running?*
• *Is a fly flying?*

Repeat the sentence, stressing the vowel sound *y* makes in each word: *The /pup/-/ē/-/ē/ ran after the /fl/-/ī/-/ī/.* Tell students that the *y* in *puppy* has the long *e* sound, and the *y* in *fly* has the long *i* sound. Point out that the words *puppy* and *fly* are in dark print.

Part B: Tell students they will write words that name pictures. Have students point to the fly and say the picture name. Then, have students point to the words in dark print in the sentence above. Ask questions that help students choose and write the word *fly*. Repeat with the picture of the puppy.

Part C: Tell students they will write the letter *y* on the line to complete the names for pictures that have either the long *e* or long *i* sound. Identify the picture of the happy boy. Have students repeat *happy*. Say the picture name again, stressing the long *e* sound: */hap/-/ē/-/ē/.* Guide students to write the letter *y*. Have students say the word again. Continue the process with the remaining pictures.

Intermediate

Part A: Follow the directions in Part A of the Beginning section, but substitute these questions:
• *What is running after the fly?*
• *What is the puppy running to?*

Part B: Tell students they will write words that name pictures. Then, help students identify the pictures. Have them complete the section with a partner.

Part C: Tell students they will write the letter *y* on the line to complete the names for pictures that have either the long *e* or long *i* sound. Identify the picture of the happy boy. Have students repeat *happy*. Say the picture name again, stressing the long *e* sound: */hap/-/ē/-/ē/.* Guide students to write the letter *y*. Have students say the word again. Help students identify the names of the remaining pictures. Ask students to work with a partner to complete the page.

Advanced

Part A: Distribute page 51. Direct students to look at the first picture. Read the sentence aloud and have students repeat it. Invite students to talk about the picture. Repeat the sentence, stressing the vowel sound *y* makes in each word: *The /pup/-/ē/-/ē/ ran after the /fl/-/ī/-/ī/.* Tell students that the *y* in *puppy* has the long *e* sound, and the *y* in *fly* has the long *i* sound. Point out that the words *puppy* and *fly* are in dark print.

Parts B and C: Read aloud the directions and identify the pictures. Have students complete the page independently.

EXTENSION

Write the following words on cards: *cry, fry, sky, city, story, body.* Display each card and read the word out loud. Have students repeat the words and tell which ending sound *y* makes.

y as a Vowel

A. Read the sentence.

The **puppy** ran after the **fly**.

B. Write the name of each picture. Use the words in dark print above.

1.

_____

2.

_____

C. Write **y** to complete the words.

3.

happ _____

4.

sk _____

5.

bunn _____

6.

cr _____

r-Controlled Vowel *ar*

NOTE: Students whose native language is Italian may have problems with the *ar* sound.

INTRODUCTION

Cut out a star from paper. Say: *This is a star.* Have students repeat the sentence. Pass the picture to each student and say: *(Name) is holding the star.* Encourage the students to repeat the sentence each time. Say *star* again, stressing the ending sound: */st/-/är/-/är/.* Tell students that /är/ is made with the letters *a* and *r.*

 Invite students to say the word *star* in their native language.

 The homograph *star* may confuse students. Explain that *star* has several meanings and identify two. Then, say simple sentences that provide context clues of the word's use. (*Lisa is a singing star. Stars shine at night.*) Invite students to clap when they hear a sentence in which *star* refers to a light in the sky.

Beginning

Part A: Distribute page 53. Direct students to look at the first picture. Read the sentence aloud and have students repeat it. Invite each student to repeat the sentence individually. Then, ask the following questions about the picture:
• *What is on the car? Point to it.*
• *Where is the star? Point to it.*
• *Is the star on the car?*
• *Is the car on the star?*

Repeat the sentence, stressing the *ar* sound in each word: *Todd paints a /st/-/är/-/är/ on the /k/-/är/-/är/.* Tell students that *star* and *car* have the *ar* sound. Point out that the words *star* and *car* are in dark print.

Part B: Tell students they will write words that name pictures. Have students point to the star and say the picture name. Then, have students point to the words in dark print in the sentence above. Ask questions that help students choose and write the word *star.* Repeat with the picture of the car.

Part C: Tell students they will write words for pictures whose names have the *ar* sound. Identify the picture of the jar. Have students repeat the

word. Say the picture name again, stressing the *ar* sound: */j/-/är/-/är/.* Tell students that *jar* is spelled *j, a, r.* Help them find the word in the list, write it on the line, and cross out the word once it is chosen. Continue the process with the remaining pictures by identifying the picture and the spelling of the name.

Intermediate

Part A: Follow the directions in Part A of the Beginning section, but substitute these questions:
• *What is on the car?*
• *Where is the star?*

Part B: Tell students they will write words that name pictures. Then, help students identify the pictures. Have them complete the section with a partner.

Part C: Tell students they will write words for pictures whose names have the *ar* sound. Have students point to each word in the box as you read them aloud. Ask students to repeat the word after you. Then, identify the picture of the jar. Help students find and write the word *jar.* Say the picture name again, stressing the *ar* sound: */j/-/är/-/är/.* Help students identify the names of the remaining pictures. Ask students to work with a partner to complete the page.

Advanced

Part A: Distribute page 53. Direct students to look at the first picture. Read the sentence aloud and have students repeat it. Invite students to talk about the picture. Repeat the sentence, stressing the *ar* sound in each word: *Todd paints a /st/-/är/-/är/ on the /k/-/är/-/är/.* Tell students that *star* and *car* have the *ar* sound. Point out that the words *star* and *car* are in dark print.

Parts B and C: Read aloud the directions and identify the pictures and words. Have students complete the page independently.

EXTENSION

Invite students to cut out stars from yellow construction paper. Then, challenge students to write words that contain the *ar* sound on them.

r-Controlled Vowel *ar*

A. Read the sentence.

Todd   paints   a   **star**   on   the   **car**.

B. Write the name of each picture. Use the words in dark print above.

1.

_____

2.

_____

C. Write the word that names the picture.

barn   shark   arm   yarn   jar   scarf

3.

_____

4.

_____

5.

_____

6.

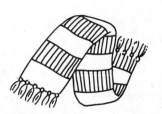

_____

7.

_____

8.

_____

r-Controlled Vowel or

INTRODUCTION

Display a can of corn or an ear of corn. Say: *This is corn.* Have students repeat the sentence. Pass the corn to each student and say: *(Name) is holding the corn.* Encourage the students to repeat the sentence each time. Say *corn* again, stressing the *or* sound: */k/-/ôr/-/ôr/-/n/.* Tell students that */ôr/* is made with the letters *o* and *r.*

 Invite students to share the word *corn* in their native language and tell their favorite way to eat it.

Beginning

Part A: Distribute page 55. Direct students to look at the first picture. Read the sentence aloud and have students repeat it. Invite each student to repeat the sentence individually. Then, ask the following questions about the picture:
• *Who eats corn? Point to it.*
• *What is the stork eating? Point to it.*
• *Is a stork eating fish?*
• *Is stork eating corn?*

Repeat the sentence, stressing the *or* sound in each word: *The /st/-/ôr/-/ôr/-/k/ eats /k/-/ôr/-/ôr/-/n/.* Tell students that *stork* and *corn* have the *or* sound. Point out that the words *stork* and *corn* are in dark print.

Part B: Tell students they will write words that name pictures. Have students point to the stork and say the picture name. Then, have students point to the words in dark print in the sentence above. Ask questions that help students choose and write the word *stork.* Repeat with the picture of the corn.

Part C: Tell students they will circle words for pictures whose names have the *or* sound. Identify the picture of the fork. Have students repeat the word. Say the picture name again, stressing the *or* sound: */f/-/ôr/-/ôr/-/k/.* Then, have students point to each word under the picture as you slowly say the words. Check that students circle the correct word. Continue the process with the remaining pictures.

Intermediate

Part A: Follow the directions in Part A of the Beginning section, but substitute these questions:
• *What is the stork eating?*
• *Who is eating corn?*

Part B: Tell students they will write words that name pictures. Then, help students identify the pictures. Have them complete the section with a partner.

Part C: Tell students they will circle words for pictures whose names have the *or* sound. Ask volunteers what picture they see. Then, have students point to each word under the picture as you read them aloud. Ask students to repeat the words after you. Check that students circle the correct word. Say the picture name again, stressing the *or* sound: */f/-/ôr/-/ôr/-/k/.* Help students identify the names of the remaining pictures and read the words. Ask students to work with a partner to complete the page.

Advanced

Part A: Distribute page 55. Direct students to look at the first picture. Read the sentence aloud and have students repeat it. Invite students to talk about the picture. Repeat the sentence, stressing the *or* sound in each word: *The /st/-/ôr/-/ôr/-/k/ eats /k/-/ôr/-/ôr/-/n/.* Tell students that *stork* and *corn* have the *or* sound. Point out that the words *stork* and *corn* are in dark print.

Parts B and C: Read aloud the directions and identify the pictures and words. Have students complete the page independently.

EXTENSION

Invite students to add kernels of corn on a large, butcher-paper corn cob. Provide students with yellow squares of paper. Challenge them to write words that have the *or* sound on the squares. Then, have students glue them to the cob. Help students read the words.

r-Controlled Vowel *or*

A. Read the sentence.

 The **stork** eats **corn**.

B. Write the name of each picture. Use the words in dark print above.

1.

_____

2.

_____

C. Circle the word that names the picture.

3.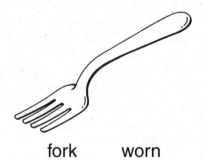

fork   worn

4.

horse   torn

5.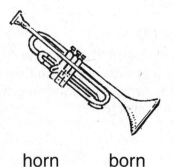

horn   born

6.

porch   torch

r-Controlled Vowels *er, ir, ur*

INTRODUCTION

Display a picture of a bird. Say: *This is a bird.* Have students repeat the sentence. Say *bird* again, stressing the middle sound: */b/-/ûr/-/ûr/-/d/.* Tell students that /ûr/ is the *er* sound. Explain that the *er* sound has several spelling patterns. Write *bird, nurse,* and *fern* on the board and underline the spelling pattern in each. Say the words as you point to them and have students repeat the words. Discuss the differences in the spelling patterns. Tell students that they will learn words that have the *er, ir,* and *ur* patterns.

 Invite students to say the word *bird* in their native language.

 As students begin to complete Part C, point out that *herd* is a homonym of *heard.* Explain the differences in the words to students.

Beginning

Part A: Distribute page 57. Direct students to look at the first picture. Read the sentence aloud and have students repeat it. Invite each student to repeat the sentence individually. Then, ask the following questions about the picture:
• *What is in the fern? Point to it.*
• *Who is looking at the bird? Point to it.*
• *Where is the bird? Point to it.*

Repeat the sentence, stressing the *er* sound in each word: *The /n/-/ûr/-/ûr/-/s/ saw a /b/-/ûr/-/ûr/-/d/ in the /f/-/ûr/-/ûr/-/n/.* Tell students that *nurse, bird,* and *fern* all have the *er* sound. Remind students of the different spelling patterns for *er.* Point out that the words *nurse, bird,* and *fern* are in dark print.

Part B: Tell students they will write words that name pictures. Have students point to the fern and say the picture name. Then, have students point to the words in dark print in the sentence above. Ask questions that help students choose and write the word *fern.* Repeat with the pictures of the nurse and bird.

Part C: Tell students they will write words for pictures whose names have the *er* sound. Identify the picture of the herd. Have students repeat the word. Say the picture name again, stressing the *er* sound: */h/-/ûr/-/ûr/-/d/.* Tell students that *herd* is spelled *h, e, r, d.* Help them find the word in the list, write it on the line, and cross out the word once it is chosen. Continue the process with the remaining pictures by identifying the picture and the spelling of the name.

Intermediate

Part A: Follow the directions in Part A of the Beginning section, but substitute these questions:
• *Is the nurse or the bird in the fern?*
• *Is the bird on the nurse or in the fern?*
• *Who sees the bird?*

Part B: Tell students they will write words that name pictures. Then, help students identify the pictures. Have them complete the section with a partner.

Part C: Tell students they will write words for pictures whose names have the *er* sound. Have students point to each word in the box as you read them aloud. Ask students to repeat the word after you. Have them identify the spelling pattern. Then, identify the picture of the herd. Help students find and write the word *herd.* Say the picture name again, stressing the *er* sound: */h/-/ûr/-/ûr/-/d/.* Help students identify the names of the remaining pictures. Ask students to work with a partner to complete the page.

Advanced

Part A: Distribute page 57. Direct students to look at the first picture. Read the sentence aloud and have students repeat it. Invite students to talk about the picture. Repeat the sentence, stressing the *er* sound in each word: *The /n/-/ûr/-/ûr/-/s/ saw a /b/-/ûr/-/ûr/-/d/ in the /f/-/ûr/-/ûr/-/n/.* Tell students that *nurse, bird,* and *fern* all have the *er* sound. Remind students of the different spelling patterns for *er.* Point out that the words *nurse, bird,* and *fern* are in dark print.

Parts B and C: Read aloud the directions and identify the pictures. Have students complete the page independently.

EXTENSION

Provide cutouts shaped like fern leaves to students. Challenge them to write words that have the *er* sound on them. Arrange the leaves together to form a branch from a fern.

Name _____ Date _____

r-Controlled Vowels *er, ir, ur*

A. Read the sentence.

The **nurse** saw a **bird** in the **fern**.

B. Write the name of each picture. Use the words in dark print above.

1.

2.

3.

_____ _____ _____

C. Write the word that names the picture.

shirt	herd	purse	girl	church	surf

4.

5.

6.

_____ _____ _____

7.

8.

9.

_____ _____ _____

s-Blends

NOTE: Students whose native language is Spanish may have problems with s-blend words.

INTRODUCTION

Take the students to the playground to look at a swing. Say: *This is a swing.* Have students repeat the sentence. Invite students to sit on the swing. Say: *(Name) sits on the swing.* Encourage students to repeat the sentence each time. Ask students to listen to the first two sounds they hear as you say the word *swing* again. Explain that the letters *s* and *w* work together to make a blend. Tell students there are other letters that work with *s* to make more blends.

 Invite students to share the word *swing* in their native language.

Beginning

Part A: Distribute page 59. Direct students to look at the first picture. Read the sentence aloud and have students repeat it. Invite each student to repeat the sentence individually. Then, ask the following questions about the picture:
• *Are two girls swinging?*
• *Is one girl sliding?*

Repeat the sentence. Tell students that *swing* is made with the blend *sw* and *slide* is made with the blend *sl*. Point out that the words *swing* and *slide* are in dark print.

Part B: Tell students they will write words that name pictures. Have students point to the slide and say the picture name. Then, have students point to the words in dark print in the sentence above. Ask questions that help students choose and write the word *slide*. Repeat with the picture of the swing.

Part C: Tell students there are many other letters that go with *s* to make other blends. Explain that they will write *s* and another letter on the lines to complete the names for pictures that have blends. Identify the picture of the spoon. Have students repeat the word. Say the picture name again, stressing the blend: /s/-/p/-/s/-/p/-/o͞on/. Guide students to write the letters as you say them. Check that students write the correct letters. Have students say the word again. Continue the process with the remaining pictures.

Intermediate

Part A: Follow the directions in Part A of the Beginning section.

Part B: Tell students they will write words that name pictures. Then, help students identify the pictures. Have them complete the section with a partner.

Part C: Tell students there are many other letters that go with *s* to make other blends. Explain that they will write *s* and another letter on the lines to complete the names for pictures that have blends. Identify the picture of the spoon. Have students repeat the word. Say the picture name again, stressing the blend: /s/-/p/-/s/-/p/-/o͞on/. Guide students to write the letters as you say them. Check that students write the correct letters. Have students say the word again. Help students identify the names of the remaining pictures. Ask students to work with a partner to complete the page.

Advanced

Part A: Distribute page 59. Direct students to look at the first picture. Read the sentence aloud and have students repeat it. Invite students to talk about the picture. Repeat the sentence. Tell students that *swing* is made with the blend *sw* and *slide* is made with the blend *sl*. Point out that the words *swing* and *slide* are in dark print.

Parts B and C: Read aloud the directions and identify the pictures. Have students complete the page independently.

EXTENSION

When on the playground, challenge students to say an s-blend word as they slide down a slide.

Name _____ Date _____

s-Blends

A. Read the sentence.

The girls **swing** and **slide**.

B. Write the name of each picture. Use the words in dark print above.

1.

_____

2.

_____

C. Write an *s*-blend to complete the words.

3.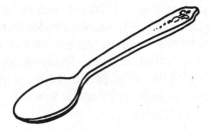

_____ _____ oon

4.

_____ _____ amp

5.

_____ _____ ake

6.

_____ _____ unk

r-Blends

NOTE: Students whose native language is Chinese, Japanese, Korean, or Vietnamese may have problems with *r*-blend words.

INTRODUCTION

Provide a grape snack for students. Say: *These are grapes.* Have students repeat the sentence. As you pass out the grapes, say: *(Name) gets some grapes.* Encourage students to repeat the sentence each time. Ask students to listen to the first two sounds they hear as you say the word *grapes* again. Explain that the letters *g* and *r* work together to make a blend. Tell students there are other letters that work with *r* to make more blends.

 Invite students to share the word *grapes* in their native language.

Beginning

Part A: Distribute page 61. Direct students to look at the first picture. Read the sentence aloud and have students repeat it. Invite each student to repeat the sentence individually. Then, ask the following questions about the picture:
• *Who is eating grapes? Point to it.*
• *What is the frog eating? Point to it.*
• *Is the frog eating hot dogs?*
• *Is the frog eating grapes?*

Repeat the sentence. Tell students that *frog* is made with the blend *fr* and *grapes* is made with the blend *gr*. Point out that the words *frog* and *grapes* are in dark print.

Part B: Tell students they will write words that name pictures. Have students point to the grapes and say the picture name. Then, have students point to the words in dark print in the sentence above. Ask questions that help students choose and write the word *grapes*. Repeat with the picture of the frog.

Part C: Tell students there are many other letters that go with *r* to make blends. Explain that they will write another letter and *r* on the lines to complete the names for pictures that have blends. Identify the picture of the tree. Have students

repeat the word. Say the picture name again, stressing the blend: /t/-/r/-/t/-/r/-/ē/. Guide students to write the letters as you say them. Check that students write the correct letters. Have students say the word again. Continue the process with the remaining pictures.

Intermediate

Part A: Follow the directions in Part A of the Beginning section.

Part B: Tell students they will write words that name pictures. Then, help students identify the pictures. Have them complete the section with a partner.

Part C: Tell students there are many other letters that go with *r* to make blends. Explain that they will write another letter and *r* on the lines to complete the names for pictures that have blends. Identify the picture of the tree. Have students repeat the word. Say the picture name again, stressing the blend: /t/-/r/-/t/-/r/-/ē/. Guide students to write the letters as you say them. Check that students write the correct letters. Have students say the word again. Help them identify the names of the remaining pictures. Ask students to work with a partner to complete the page.

Advanced

Part A: Distribute page 61. Direct students to look at the first picture. Read the sentence aloud and have students repeat it. Invite students to talk about the picture. Repeat the sentence. Tell students that *frog* is made with the blend *fr* and *grapes* is made with the blend *gr*. Point out that the words *frog* and *grapes* are in dark print.

Parts B and C: Read aloud the directions and identify the pictures. Have students complete the page independently.

E X T E N S I O N

Invite students to write *r*-blend words on green circles. Glue the circles together on butcher paper to form a bunch of grapes.

Name _____ Date _____

r-Blends

A. Read the sentence.

The **frog** eats **grapes**.

B. Write the name of each picture. Use the words in dark print above.

1.

_____

2.

_____

C. Write an *r*-blend to complete the words.

3.

_____ _____ ee

4.

_____ _____ ab

5.
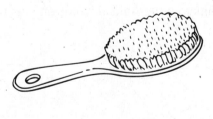

_____ _____ ush

6.

_____ _____ ice

l-Blends

NOTE: Students whose native language is Chinese, Italian, Japanese, Korean, or Vietnamese may have problems with *l*-blend words.

INTRODUCTION

Display a colorful plate. Say: *This is a plate.* Have students repeat the sentence. Pass the plate to each student and say: *(Name) has the plate.* Encourage students to repeat the sentence each time. Ask students to listen to the first two sounds they hear as you say the word *plate* again. Explain that the letters *p* and *l* work together to make a blend. Tell students there are other letters that work with *l* to make more blends.

 Invite students to share the word *plate* in their native language.

Beginning

Part A: Distribute page 63. Direct students to look at the first picture. Read the sentence aloud and have students repeat it. Invite each student to repeat the sentence individually. Then, ask the following questions about the picture:
• *What is Dan wearing to wash the plate? Point to them.*
• *What is Dan washing? Point to it.*
• *Is Dan washing a glass?*
• *Is Dan wearing gloves?*

Repeat the sentence. Tell students that *gloves* is made with the blend *gl* and *plate* is made with the blend *pl*. Point out that the words *gloves* and *plate* are in dark print.

Part B: Tell students they will write words that name pictures. Have students point to the gloves and say the picture name. Then, have students point to the words in dark print in the sentence above. Ask questions that help students choose and write the word *gloves*. Repeat with the picture of the plate.

Part C: Tell students there are many other letters that go with *l* to make blends. Explain that they will write another letter and *l* on the lines to complete the names for pictures that have blends. Identify the picture of the clown. Have students

repeat the word. Say the picture name again, stressing the blend: /k/-/l/-/k/-/l/-/oun/. Guide students to write the letters as you say them. Check that students write the correct letters. Have students say the word again. Continue the process with the remaining pictures.

Intermediate

Part A: Follow the directions in Part A of the Beginning section.

Part B: Tell students they will write words that name pictures. Then, help students identify the pictures. Have them complete the section with a partner.

Part C: Tell students there are many other letters that go with *l* to make blends. Explain that they will write another letter and *l* on the lines to complete the names for pictures that have blends. Identify the picture of the clown. Have students repeat the word. Say the picture name again, stressing the blend: /k/-/l/-/k/-/l/-/oun/. Guide students to write the letters as you say them. Check that students write the correct letters. Have students say the word again. Help them identify the names of the remaining pictures. Ask students to work with a partner to complete the page.

Advanced

Part A: Distribute page 63. Direct students to look at the first picture. Read the sentence aloud and have students repeat it. Invite students to talk about the picture. Repeat the sentence. Tell students that *gloves* is made with the blend *gl* and *plate* is made with the blend *pl*. Point out that the words *gloves* and *plate* are in dark print.

Parts B and C: Read aloud the directions and identify the pictures and words. Have students complete the page independently.

EXTENSION

Invite students to write *l*-blend words on paper plates.

Name _____   Date _____

l-Blends

A. Read the sentence.

Dan wears **gloves** to wash the **plate**.

B. Write the name of each picture. Use the words in dark print above.

1.

_____

2.

_____

C. Write an *l*-blend to complete the words.

3.

____ ____ own

4.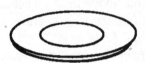

____ ____ ute

5.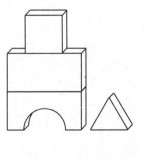

____ ____ ocks

6.

____ ____ ue

Sounds of c

INTRODUCTION

Display a picture of a city. Say: *This is a city.* Have students repeat the sentence. Repeat with a picture of a cat. Write *city* and *cat* on the board. Underline the letter *c* in each word. Explain that the letter *c* can have two sounds. Tell students they will hear /s/ when *c* is before *e, i,* or *y.* They will hear /k/ when *c* is before any other letter.

 Invite students to describe the things they would find in a city in their native country.

Beginning

Part A: Distribute page 65. Direct students to look at the first picture. Read the sentence aloud and have students repeat it. Invite each student to repeat the sentence individually. Then, ask the following questions about the picture:
• *Where is the cat? Point to it.*
• *What animal is in the city? Point to it.*
• *Is a dog in the city?*
• *Is a cat in the city?*

Repeat the sentence. Remind students that *c* makes the /s/ sound before the letters *e, i,* or *y,* and the /k/ sound before any other letter. Point out that the words *cat* and *city* are in dark print.

Part B: Tell students they will write words that name pictures. Have students point to the city and say the picture name. Then, have students point to the words in dark print in the sentence above. Ask questions that help students choose and write the word *city.* Repeat with the picture of the cat.

Part C: Tell students they will write words for pictures whose names have the /k/ or /s/ sound for the letter *c.* Identify the picture of the fence. Have students repeat the word. Say the picture name again, stressing the /s/ sound: */fen/-/s/-/s/.* Explain that in this word the *c* is at the end of the word. Tell students that *fence* is spelled *f, e, n, c, e.* Help them find the word in the list, write it on the line, and cross out the word once it is chosen. Ask what letter follows *c.* Continue the process with the remaining pictures by identifying the picture and the spelling of the name.

Intermediate

Part A: Follow the directions in Part A of the Beginning section.

Part B: Tell students they will write words that name pictures. Then, help students identify the pictures. Have them complete the section with a partner.

Part C: Tell students they will write words for pictures whose names have the /k/ or /s/ sound for the letter *c.* Have students point to each word in the box as you read them aloud. Ask students to repeat the word after you. Have them identify the letter that follows *c.* Then, identify the picture of the fence. Help students find and write the word *fence.* Say the picture name again, stressing the /s/ sound: */fen/-/s/-/s/.* Help students identify the names of the remaining pictures. Ask students to work with a partner to complete the page.

Advanced

Part A: Distribute page 65. Direct students to look at the first picture. Read the sentence aloud and have students repeat it. Invite students to talk about the picture. Repeat the sentence. Remind students that *c* makes the /s/ sound before the letters *e, i,* or *y,* and the /k/ sound before any other letter. Point out that the words *cat* and *city* are in dark print.

Parts B and C: Read aloud the directions and identify the pictures and words. Have students complete the page independently.

EXTENSION

Invite students to make rubbings of the front and back of a penny using a crayon. Write *cent* and *crayon* on the board and underline the *c* in each word. Ask students which letters follow the *c* and review the rules for when *c* makes the /k/ or /s/ sound.

Sounds of *c*

A. Read the sentence.

The **cat** lives in the **city**.

B. Write the name of each picture. Use the words in dark print above.

1.

_____

2.

_____

C. Write the word that names the picture.

cup pencil face can cut fence

3.

_____

4.

_____

5.

_____

6.
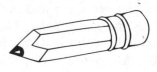

_____

7.

_____

8.

_____

Sounds of *g*

NOTE: Students whose native language is Chinese, French, Greek, or Spanish may have problems with the /g/ or /j/ sounds.

INTRODUCTION

Display a picture of a garden. Say: *This is a garden.* Have students repeat the sentence. Repeat with a picture of a gerbil. Write *garden* and *gerbil* on the board. Underline the letter *g* in each word. Explain that the letter *g* can have two sounds. Tell students they will hear /j/ when *g* is before *e, i,* or *y.* They will hear /g/ when *g* is before any other letter.

 Invite students to describe the fruits and vegetables they would find in a garden in their native country.

Beginning

Part A: Distribute page 67. Direct students to look at the first picture. Read the sentence aloud and have students repeat it. Invite each student to repeat the sentence individually. Then, ask the following questions about the picture:
• *Where is the gerbil? Point to it.*
• *What is in the garden? Point to it.*
• *Is the gerbil in a garden?*
• *Is the gerbil in a wagon?*

Repeat the sentence. Remind students that *g* makes the /j/ sound before the letters *e, i,* or *y,* and the /g/ sound before any other letter. Point out that the words *gerbil* and *garden* are in dark print.

Part B: Tell students they will write words that name pictures. Have students point to the garden and say the picture name. Then, have students point to the words in dark print in the sentence above. Ask questions that help students choose and write the word *garden.* Repeat with the picture of the gerbil.

Part C: Tell students they will write words for pictures whose names have the /g/ or /j/ sound for the letter *g.* Identify the picture of the giraffe. Have students repeat the word. Say the picture name again, stressing the /j/ sound: */j/-/j/-/ji/-/raf/.* Tell students that *giraffe* is spelled *g, i, ,r, a, f, f, e.* Help

them find the word in the list, write it on the line, and cross out the word once it is chosen. Ask what letter follows *g.* Continue the process with the remaining pictures by identifying the picture and the spelling of the name.

Intermediate

Part A: Follow the directions in Part A of the Beginning section.

Part B: Tell students they will write words that name pictures. Then, help students identify the pictures. Have them complete the section with a partner.

Part C: Tell students they will write words for pictures whose names have the /g/ or /j/ sound for the letter *g.* Have students point to each word in the box as you read them aloud. Ask students to repeat the word after you. Have them identify the letter that follows *g.* Then, identify the picture of the giraffe. Help students find and write the word *giraffe.* Say the picture name again, stressing the /j/ sound: */j/-/j/-/ji/-/raf/.* Help students identify the names of the remaining pictures. Ask students to work with a partner to complete the page.

Advanced

Part A: Distribute page 67. Direct students to look at the first picture. Read the sentence aloud and have students repeat it. Invite students to talk about the picture. Repeat the sentence. Remind students that *g* makes the /j/ sound before the letters *e, i,* or *y,* and the /g/ sound before any other letter. Point out that the words *gerbil* and *garden* are in dark print.

Parts B and C: Read aloud the directions and identify the pictures and words. Have students complete the page independently.

EXTENSION

Challenge students to solve riddles. Give clues about one of the pictures on page 67 for students to solve. The student who solves it then tells a new riddle.

Name _____   Date _____

Sounds of *g*

A. Read the sentence.

   The **gerbil** is in the **garden**.

B. Write the name of each picture. Use the words in dark print above.

1.

_____

2.

_____

C. Write the word that names the picture.

gum   giant   giraffe   dog   cage   goat

3.

_____

4.

_____

5.

_____

6.

_____

7.

_____

8.

_____

Sounds of *s*

NOTE: Students whose native language is Chinese, French, Greek, Japanese, Korean, Spanish, Urdu, or Vietnamese may have problems with /s/, /z/, or /sh/ sounds.

INTRODUCTION

Write *seal* on the board and underline the *s*. Explain that a seal is an animal and remind students that *seal* begins with the /s/ sound. Then, display a box of tissues. Pretend to blow your nose. Say: *I use a tissue to blow my nose.* Have students repeat the sentence. Write *nose* and *tissue* on the board. Underline the letters *s* or *ss* in each word. Explain that the letter *s* can also have the /z/ sound in *nose* and the /sh/ sound in *tissue*.

 Invite students to say *nose* in their native language.

Beginning

Part A: Distribute page 69. Direct students to look at the first picture. Read the sentence aloud and have students repeat it. Invite each student to repeat the sentence individually. Then, ask the following questions about the picture:
• *What is the seal blowing? Point to it.*
• *What is the seal using on his nose? Point to it.*
• *What has the tissue? Point to it.*

Repeat the sentence. Remind students that *s* makes the /s/, /z/, and /sh/ sounds. Point out that the words *seal, nose,* and *tissue* are in dark print.

Part B: Tell students they will write words that name pictures. Have students point to the tissue and say the picture name. Then, have students point to the words in dark print in the sentence above. Ask questions that help students choose and write the word *tissue*. Repeat with the pictures of the seal and the nose.

Part C: Tell students they will write *s, z,* or *sh* to show the sound for *s* in words. Identify the picture of the soap. Have students repeat the word. Say the picture name again, stressing the /s/ sound: */s/-/s/-/ōp/*. Have them write *s* on the line. Continue the process with the remaining pictures by identifying the picture and the sound for *s*.

Intermediate

Part A: Follow the directions in Part A of the Beginning section.

Part B: Tell students they will write words that name pictures. Then, help students identify the pictures. Have them complete the section with a partner.

Part C: Tell students they will write *s, z,* or *sh* to show the sound for *s* in words. Have students point to the picture of the soap. Ask students to repeat the word after you. Say the picture name again, stressing the /s/ sound: */s/-/s/-/ōp/*. Have them write *s* on the line. Help students identify the names of the remaining pictures. Ask students to work with a partner to complete the page.

Advanced

Part A: Distribute page 69. Direct students to look at the first picture. Read the sentence aloud and have students repeat it. Invite students to talk about the picture. Repeat the sentence. Remind students that *s* makes the /s/, /z/, and /sh/ sounds. Point out that the words *seal, nose,* and *tissue* are in dark print.

Parts B and C: Read aloud the directions and identify the pictures and words. Have students complete the page independently.

E X T E N S I O N

Invite students to write sentences with words that contain the /s/, /z/, or /sh/ sound for *s*. Challenge them to use as many words in the same sentence as possible.

Name _____ Date _____

Sounds of *s*

A. Read the sentence.

The **seal** blew his **nose** on a **tissue**.

B. Write the name of each picture. Use the words in dark print above.

1.

_____

2.

_____

3.

_____

C. Write **s**, **z**, or **sh** on the line to tell the sound that *s* makes in each picture name.

4.
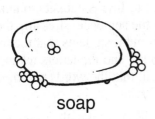

soap

_____

5.

hose

_____

6.

mission

_____

7.

sugar

_____

8.
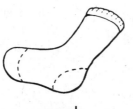

sock

_____

9.

music

_____

Digraphs *ch* and *wh*

NOTE: Students whose native language is Chinese, French, Greek, Japanese, or Spanish may have problems with *ch* and *wh* words.

INTRODUCTION

Invite students to play telephone. Tell them you will say one word that they are to share with others one at a time. Then, whisper *children* in one student's ear and have the person pass the message to another student. After the last student has shared the word, point out that students were whispering. Write *whisper* and *children* on the board and underline *wh* and *ch*. Explain that *wh* has the /wh/ sound in *whisper* and *ch* has the /ch/ sound in *children*.

 Invite students to play telephone again by whispering the word *children* in their native language.

Beginning

Part A: Distribute page 71. Direct students to look at the first picture. Read the sentence aloud and have students repeat it. Invite each student to whisper the sentence. Then, ask the following questions about the picture:
• *What are the children doing? Show me.*
• *Who is whispering? Point to them.*
• *Are the children yelling?*
• *Are the children whispering?*

Repeat the sentence, stressing the /ch/ and /wh/ sounds. Remind students that the letters *ch* make the /ch/ sound and the letters *wh* make the /wh/ sound. Point out that the words *children* and *whisper* are in dark print.

Part B: Tell students they will write words that name pictures. Have students point to the children and say the picture name. Then, have students point to the words in dark print in the sentence above. Ask questions that help students choose and write the word *children*. Repeat with the picture that shows a whisper.

Part C: Tell students they will write *ch* or *wh* to show the sound they hear at the beginning of

picture names. Identify the picture of the chair. Have students repeat the word. Say the picture name again, stressing the /ch/ sound: /ch/-/ch/-/är/. Have them write *ch* on the line. Continue the process with the remaining pictures by identifying the picture and the sound at the beginning of the picture name.

Intermediate

Part A: Follow the directions in Part A of the Beginning section, but substitute these questions:
• *What are the children doing?*
• *Who is whispering?*

Part B: Tell students they will write words that name pictures. Then, help students identify the pictures. Have them complete the section with a partner.

Part C: Tell students they will write *ch* or *wh* to show the sound they hear at the beginning of picture names. Identify the picture of the chair. Have students repeat the word. Say the picture name again, stressing the /ch/ sound: /ch/-/ch/-/är/. Have them write *ch* on the line. Help students identify the names of the remaining pictures. Ask students to work with a partner to complete the page.

Advanced

Part A: Distribute page 71. Direct students to look at the first picture. Read the sentence aloud and have students repeat it. Invite students to talk about the picture. Repeat the sentence, stressing the /ch/ and /wh/ sounds. Remind students that the letters *ch* make the /ch/ sound and the letters *wh* make the /wh/ sound. Point out that the words *children* and *whisper* are in dark print.

Parts B and C: Read aloud the directions and identify the pictures. Have students complete the page independently.

EXTENSION

Invite students to play telephone again. Challenge them to send messages in which a sentence has both a word that begins with *ch* and *wh*.

Digraphs *ch* and *wh*

A. Read the sentence.

 The **children** **whisper** quietly.

B. Write the name of each picture. Use the words in dark print above.

1.

_____

2.

_____

C. Write **ch** or **wh** on the line to tell the beginning sound in each picture name.

3.

_____

4.

_____

5.

_____

6.

_____

7.

_____

8.

_____

Digraphs *sh* and *th*

NOTE: Students whose native language is Chinese, French, Italian, Japanese, Korean, Urdu, or Vietnamese may have problems with *sh* and *th* words.

INTRODUCTION

Invite a student wearing a brightly colored shirt to stand. Say: *I think that shirt is [color].* Have students repeat the sentence. Write *shirt* on the board and underline *sh*. Explain that the letters *sh* have the /sh/ sound in *shirt*. Next, write *think* and *that* on the board. Underline *th* in each word. Point out that *th* can have two sounds. Tell students it can have the whispered /th/ in *think* and the voiced /th/ in *that*. Repeat each word several times for students to listen to the initial sounds.

 Invite students to name the clothes they are wearing in their native language.

 Note that some students may have trouble hearing the different vowel sounds in the words *sheep* and *ship* in Part C.

Beginning

Part A: Distribute page 73. Direct students to look at the first picture. Read the sentence aloud and have students repeat it. Invite each student to repeat the sentence individually. Then, ask the following questions about the picture:
• *What is the girl looking at? Point to it.*
• *How much does the shirt cost? Point to it.*
• *Is the girl looking at that shirt?*
• *Is that shirt thirteen dollars?*

Repeat the sentence, stressing the /th/ and /sh/ sounds. Remind students that the letters *th* make the beginning sounds in *that* and *thirteen*, and the letters *sh* make the beginning sound in *shirt*. Point out that the words *that, shirt,* and *thirteen* are in dark print.

Part B: Tell students they will write words that name pictures. Have students point to the shirt and say the picture name. Then, have students point to the words in dark print in the sentence above. Ask questions that help students choose and write the word *shirt*. Repeat with the pictures that show *that* and *thirteen*.

Part C: Tell students they will write *sh* or *th* to show the sound they hear at the beginning of

picture names. Identify the picture of the sheep. Have students repeat the word. Say the picture name again, stressing the /sh/ sound: /sh/-/sh/-/ēp/. Have them write *sh* on the line. Continue the process with the remaining pictures by identifying the picture and the sound at the beginning of the picture name.

Intermediate

Part A: Follow the directions in Part A of the Beginning section, but substitute these questions:
• *What is the girl looking at?*
• *How much does that shirt cost?*

Part B: Tell students they will write words that name pictures. Then, help students identify the pictures. Have them complete the section with a partner.

Part C: Tell students they will write *sh* or *th* to show the sound they hear at the beginning of picture names. Identify the picture of the sheep. Have students repeat the word. Say the picture name again, stressing the /sh/ sound: /sh/-/sh/-/ēp/. Have them write *sh* on the line. Help students identify the names of the remaining pictures. Ask students to work with a partner to complete the page.

Advanced

Part A: Distribute page 73. Direct students to look at the first picture. Read the sentence aloud and have students repeat it. Invite students to talk about the picture. Repeat the sentence, stressing the /sh/ and /th/ sounds. Remind students that the letters *th* make the beginning sounds in *that* and *thirteen*, and the letters *sh* make the beginning sound in *shirt*. Point out that the words *that, shirt,* and *thirteen* are in dark print.

Parts B and C: Read aloud the directions and identify the pictures. Have students complete the page independently.

EXTENSION

Write the words *this, that, these,* and *those* on cards. Explain that many words that begin with the digraph *th* tell where things are. Pass out the cards to students, and have them use the words in sentences to tell the relative location of items in the classroom. (*I like this book.*)

Name _____   Date _____

Digraphs *sh* and *th*

A. Read the sentence.

That **shirt** is **thirteen** dollars.

B. Write the name of each picture. Use the words in dark print above.

1.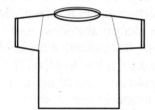

_____

2.

_____

3.

_____

C. Write **sh** or **th** on the line to tell the beginning sound in each picture name.

4.

_____

5.

_____

6.

_____

7.

_____

8.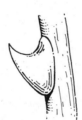

_____

9.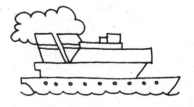

_____

Unit 2: Phonics
ESL 2-3, SV 7097-1

Naming Words

INTRODUCTION

Write the column headings *Person, Place,* and *Thing* on the board. Invite students to name kinds of people. Write each name on the board as it is identified. Repeat the process with the other two heads. Tell students that the words on the board are naming words, or nouns. Explain that naming words tell about a person, place, or thing.

 Invite students to compare specific places in the United States, such as stores, with those in their native country.

Beginning

Part A: Distribute page 75. Direct students to look at the first picture. Read the sentence aloud and have students repeat it. Ask the following questions about the picture:
• *Who is at the farm? Point to it.*
• *What is the boy feeding? Point to it.*
• *Is the goat at the farm?*

Tell students that *boy, goat,* and *farm* are naming words. Remind students that naming words tell about a person, place, or thing.

Part B: Tell students they will write the words in dark print on lines to tell if they name a person, place, or thing. Have students point to the word *boy* and repeat it. Ask questions that help students decide if the word names a person, place, or thing. Guide them to write it in on the correct line. Repeat with the remaining words.

Part C: Tell students they will draw lines from pictures to tell if the picture names a person, place, or thing. Identify the picture of the book and have students repeat the word. Help them realize that *book* names a thing. Guide them to draw a line between the book and the word *thing.* Continue the process with the remaining pictures.

Intermediate

Part A: Follow the directions in Part A of the Beginning section, but substitute these questions:
• *Who is at the farm?*
• *What is the boy feeding?*
• *Where does a goat live?*

Part B: Tell students they will write the words in dark print on lines to tell if they name a person, place, or thing. Have students point to the word *boy* and repeat it. Ask questions that help students decide if the word names a person, place, or thing. Guide them to write it in on the correct line. Review the remaining words in dark print and have students complete the section.

Part C: Tell students they will draw lines from pictures to tell if the picture names a person, place, or thing. Help students identify the book. Ask questions that help them determine that the book is a thing. Guide them to draw a line to *thing.* Identify the remaining pictures and pause to allow students to draw lines to show their answers.

Advanced

Part A: Distribute page 75. Direct students to look at the first picture. Read the sentence aloud and have students repeat it. Invite students to talk about the picture. Tell students that *boy, goat,* and *farm* are naming words. Remind students that naming words are words that tell about a person, place, or thing.

Parts B and C: Read aloud the directions and identify the words and pictures. Have students complete the page independently.

EXTENSION

Refer to the list of nouns compiled on the board. Challenge each student to say a sentence that names a person, place, and thing.

Name _____   Date _____

Naming Words

A. Read the sentence.

   The **boy** feeds a **goat** at the **farm**.

B. Read each word in dark print. Does the word name a person, a place, or a thing? Write it on the line.

1.   person   **2.**   place   **3.**   thing

_____   _____   _____

C. Draw lines to show if the picture is a person, place, or thing.

4.

5.

6.

person   place   thing

7.

8.

9.

Special Names

INTRODUCTION

Invite a volunteer to stand. Say: *(Name) is a (girl/boy)*. Write the student's name and gender on the board. Explain to students that some words name a special person, place, or thing and that these nouns begin with capital letters. Explain that the name on the board is a special noun, or proper noun, and the word *boy/girl* is a common noun. Guide students to understand the difference.

Beginning

Part A: Distribute page 77. Direct students to look at the first picture. Read the sentence aloud and have students repeat it. Ask the following questions about the picture:
• *Is the name of the boy Marco?*
• *Does Marco live on South Street?*

Tell students that *Marco* and *South Street* are special nouns that begin with capital letters. Remind students that nouns are words that name a person, place, or thing.

Part B: Tell students they will write the special names in dark print on lines to tell what kind of noun they are. Have students point to and say the word *boy*. Guide them to find the word in dark print that names a boy and write it on the line. Repeat with the word *street*.

Part C: Tell students they will underline words that name special people, places, or things in sentences. Read aloud the first sentence. Have students repeat it. Help them realize that *Marco* is the special name of a person and have them underline the name. Continue the process with the remaining sentences.

Intermediate

Part A: Follow the directions in Part A of the Beginning section, but substitute these questions:
• *What is the name of the boy?*
• *On what street does the boy live?*

Part B: Tell students they will write the special names in dark print on lines to tell what kind of noun they are. Have students point to and say the nouns. Review the words in dark print and have students complete the section independently.

Part C: Tell students they will underline words that name special people, places, or things in sentences. Read aloud the first sentence. Have students repeat it. Ask questions that help them determine that *Marco* is the special name. Guide them to underline *Marco*. Read the remaining sentences and pause to allow students to underline their answers.

Advanced

Part A: Distribute page 77. Direct students to look at the first picture. Read the sentence aloud and have students repeat it. Invite students to talk about the picture. Ask students how they know that *Marco* and *South Street* are special names, or proper nouns. Remind students that nouns are words that name a person, place, or thing.

Parts B and C: Read aloud the directions, the words, and sentences. Have students complete the page independently.

EXTENSION

Have students draw a picture of their family. Help them label the people with proper nouns.

Name _____   Date _____

Special Names

A. Read the sentence.

   **Marco** lives on **South Street**.

B. Read each word in dark print. What kind of noun is it? Write it on the line.

1.   boy   **2.**   street

_____   _____

C. Draw a line under the proper noun in each sentence.

3. Marco walks to the store.

4. The store is on Main Street.

5. It is near Stone Library.

6. He buys a book for Emily.

More Than One

INTRODUCTION

Display a box of crayons. Hold up one crayon and say: *I have one crayon.* Have students repeat the sentence. Then, hold up two crayons. Say: *I have two crayons.* Write *crayon* and *crayons* on the board. Say each word and show the corresponding number of crayons. Underline the *s* in *crayons* and explain that *crayon* is a noun; it names a thing. Tell students that words that mean more than one usually end in *s*. Reinforce the skill by saying one of the words and having volunteers hold up the corresponding number of crayons as they repeat the word. Repeat with empty boxes to introduce that *es* is added to words ending in *x, ss, ch,* or *sh.*

Beginning

Part A: Distribute page 79. Direct students to look at the first picture. Read the sentence aloud and have students repeat it. Ask the following questions about the picture:
• *How many logs do you see? Hold up the number of fingers to show me.*
• *How many frogs do you see? Hold up the number of fingers to show me.*

Have students circle the words *frogs* and *log.* Point out that both words are naming words, or nouns. Explain to students that *frogs* means more than one frog because it ends in *s*. Point out that *log* means only one.

Part B: Tell students they will write the words in dark print on lines to show which word names one and which word names more than one. Read the word *log.* Have students point to it and repeat it. Ask questions that help students realize that since there is no *s* on *log,* it is not a plural noun. Guide them to write it on the line labeled *one.* Read the word *frogs.* Have students point to it and repeat it. Ask questions that help students realize that since there is an *s* on *frogs,* it is a plural noun. Guide them to write it on the line labeled *more than one.*

Part C: Tell students they will write words to name more than one. Identify the picture of the books and have students repeat the word. Help them realize that there is more than one book. Ask questions that help them write the word *books.* Continue the process with the remaining pictures and words.

Intermediate

Part A: Follow the directions in Part A of the Beginning section, but substitute these questions:
• *Do you see one or two frogs?*
• *Do you see one or two logs?*

Part B: Tell students they will write the words in dark print on lines to show which word names one and which word names more than one. Read the words *frogs* and *log.* Have students point to the words and repeat them. Ask questions that help students realize that because *frogs* ends in *s*, it is a plural noun. Have students complete the section.

Part C: Tell students they will write words to name more than one. Identify the picture of the books and have students repeat the word. Help them realize that there is more than one book. Ask questions that help them write the word *books.* Remind students that they should add *es* to words ending in *x, ss, ch,* or *sh.* Then, identify the remaining pictures and pause to allow students to write their answers.

Advanced

Part A: Distribute page 79. Direct students to look at the first picture. Read the sentence aloud and have students repeat it. Invite students to talk about the picture. Tell students that *frogs* and *log* are naming words, or nouns. Explain to students that *frogs* means more than one frog because it ends in *s*. Point out that *log* means only one.

Parts B and C: Read aloud the directions and identify the pictures and words. Remind students that they should add *es* to words ending in *x, ss, ch,* or *sh.* Have students complete the page independently.

EXTENSION

Invite partners to go on a scavenger hunt to find groups of items. Help students name and label their items. Ask students to underline the *s* or *es* ending.

Name _____   Date _____

More Than One

A. Read the sentence.

The **frogs** sit on a **log**.

B. Read each word in dark print. Does the word name one or more than one?
Write the word on the line.

1.   one   **2.**   more than one

_____   _____

C. Write the words to make them name more than one.

3.

book _____

4.

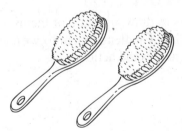

brush _____

5.

tree _____

Action Words

INTRODUCTION

Whisper actions in volunteers' ears that they will pantomime. You might have students jump, kick, or run in place. Write each action word on the board as it is named. Tell students that the volunteers are showing actions.

 Invite students to say an action word in their native language and to act it out. Have the others guess the movement.

Beginning

Part A: Distribute page 81. Direct students to look at the first picture. Read the sentence aloud and have students repeat it. Ask the following questions about the picture:
• *What does the boy do with his feet? Show me.*
• *What does the boy do with his hand? Show me.*

Tell students that *walks* and *waves* are action words, or verbs. Have them repeat the words as they pantomime the movements.

Part B: Tell students they will write the words in dark print that name actions. Have students point to the hand waving and say the action. Then, have students point to the words in dark print in the sentence above. Ask questions that help students choose and write the word *waves*. Repeat with the picture of the feet walking.

Part C: Tell students they will write action words that complete sentences. Slowly read the action words in the box as students point to them and repeat them. Pantomime each word. Then, identify the picture of the sleeping cat. Read the sentence and substitute each action word. Guide students to write *sleeps* on the line and mark it out in the box. Continue the process with the remaining pictures.

Intermediate

Part A: Follow the directions in Part A of the Beginning section, but substitute these questions:
• *What does the boy do with his feet?*
• *What does the boy do with his hand?*

Part B: Tell students they will write the words in dark print that name actions. Have students identify the actions. Then, have students point to and read the words in dark print in the sentence above. Have them complete the section independently.

Part C: Tell students they will write action words that complete sentences. Slowly read the action words in the box as students point to them and repeat them. Then, identify the picture of the sleeping cat. Read the sentence and substitute each action word. Guide students to write *sleeps* on the line and mark it out in the box. Read aloud the remaining sentences and pause to allow students to write their answers.

Advanced

Part A: Distribute page 81. Direct students to look at the first picture. Read the sentence aloud and have students repeat it. Invite students to talk about the picture. Tell students that *walks* and *waves* are action words, or verbs.

Parts B and C: Read aloud the directions. Identify the words and read the sentences. Have students complete the page independently.

EXTENSION

Invite students to draw a picture of themselves doing something. Challenge them to write a sentence that names the action.

Name _____   Date _____

Action Words

A. Read the sentence.

The boy **walks** and **waves**.

B. Write the name of each picture. Use the words in dark print above.

1.

_____

2.

_____

C. Write a word from the box to complete the sentence.

jump	sleeps	swims

3.

The cat _____.

4.

The children _____.

5.

The shark _____.

Adding *ed*

INTRODUCTION

Ask students if they talked on the phone yesterday. Invite volunteers to tell whom they talked with: *I talked with (name).* Write *talked* on the board. Explain that *ed* is added to the end of most words to show an action that happened in the past. Challenge students to name other actions they did yesterday and write the words ending in *ed* on the board.

 Invite students to use their native language to tell about something they did yesterday and to pantomime it for others to guess.

Beginning

Part A: Distribute page 83. Direct students to look at the first picture. Read the sentence aloud and have students repeat it. Ask the following questions about the picture:
• *What did Ben do yesterday? Show me.*
• *Does the picture show that Ben talked?*
• *Does the picture show that Ben skated?*

Tell students that *skated* is an action word. Remind them that the *ed* ending is a clue that the action happened in the past.

Part B: Tell students they will write words to show actions that happened in the past. Have students point to the word *climb*. Read it out loud and have students repeat it. Then, tell students they need to rewrite the words to show the action happened yesterday. Ask questions that help students rewrite the word and add *ed*. Repeat with the word *pull*.

Part C: Tell students they will circle words that show past actions to complete sentences. Explain that each sentence has two words they can choose from and that you will read the sentence twice so they can hear each choice. Read the sentence and substitute each word choice. Ask questions that help children recognize that the *ed* ending is a clue. Continue the process with the remaining sentences.

Intermediate

Part A: Follow the directions in Part A of the Beginning section, but substitute this question:
• *What did Ben do yesterday?*

Part B: Tell students they will write words to show actions that happened in the past. Have students identify the actions. Then, have students point to and read the word *climb*. Ask questions that help students rewrite the word and add *ed*. Have them write the last word independently.

Part C: Tell students they will circle words that show past actions to complete sentences. Explain that each sentence has two words they can choose from. Read the sentence and substitute each word choice. Ask questions that help children recognize that the *ed* ending is a clue. Read aloud the remaining sentences, but not the choices, and pause to allow students to circle their answers.

Advanced

Part A: Distribute page 83. Direct students to look at the first picture. Read the sentence aloud and have students repeat it. Invite students to talk about the picture. Tell students that *skated* is an action word. Remind them that the *ed* ending is a clue that the action happened in the past.

Parts B and C: Read aloud the directions, words, and sentences. Have students complete the page independently.

EXTENSION

Pair students and have them tell activities they participated in yesterday.

Name _____   Date _____

Adding *ed*

A. Read the sentence.

Ben **skated** yesterday.

B. Write the word to show that it happened yesterday.

1.

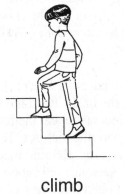

climb

_____

2.

pull

_____

C. Make each sentence tell about the past. Circle the correct word.

3. Ben (visits, visited) a friend yesterday.

4. They (played, plays) games.

5. They (walks, walked) to the park.

Is or Are

INTRODUCTION

Show students a red crayon. Say: *This crayon is red.* Then, show students two blue crayons. Say: *These crayons are blue.* Write *is* and *are* on the board. Say them and have students repeat the words. Explain that some verbs do not show action. Guide students to understand that *is* and *are* tell about something that is happening now. Point out that *is* tells about one person, place, or thing, while *are* tells about more than one person, place, or thing.

Beginning

Part A: Distribute page 85. Direct students to look at the pictures of the birds. Read the sentences aloud and have students repeat them. Ask the following questions about the pictures:
• *Which picture shows one bird? Point to it.*
• *Look at the word in dark print. Do you see* is?
• *Which picture shows three birds? Point to it.*
• *Look at the word in dark print. Do you see* are?

Tell students that *is* and *are* are verbs. Remind them that *is* will be used when the sentence tells about one person, place, or thing. Explain that *are* will be used when the sentence tells about more than one person, place, or thing.

Part B: Tell students they will write *is* or *are* in sentences. Direct students to look at the first picture. Ask how many frogs they see. Then, read aloud the first sentence and have them repeat it. Guide students to write *are* on the line. Repeat with the next picture and sentence.

Part C: Tell students they will circle *is* or *are* to complete sentences. Explain that each sentence has two words they can choose from and that you will read the sentence twice so they can hear each choice. Read the sentence and substitute each word choice. Ask questions about the number of things to help students choose the correct word. Continue the process with the remaining sentences.

Intermediate

Part A: Follow the directions in Part A of the Beginning section, but substitute these questions:
• *How many birds do you see in the first picture?*
• *What is the word in dark print under that picture?*
• *How many birds do you see in the second picture?*
• *What is the word in dark print under that picture?*

Part B: Follow the directions in Part B of the Beginning section.

Part C: Tell students they will circle *is* or *are* to complete sentences. Explain that each sentence has two words they can choose from. Read the sentence and substitute each word choice. Ask questions about the number of things to help students choose the correct word. Read aloud the remaining sentences, but not the choices, and pause to allow students to circle their answers.

Advanced

Part A: Distribute page 85. Direct students to look at the pictures of the birds. Read the sentences aloud and have students repeat them. Invite students to talk about the pictures. Tell students that *is* and *are* are verbs. Remind them that *is* will be used when the sentence tells about one person, place, or thing. Explain that *are* will be used when the sentence tells about more than one person, place, or thing.

Parts B and C: Read aloud the directions. Read aloud the sentences. Have students complete the page independently.

EXTENSION

Look for opportunities throughout the day where students use *is* and *are* in context and point out the examples.

Is or Are

A. Read the sentences.

The bird **is** on the fence.

The birds **are** on the fence.

B. Write **is** or **are** to complete the sentence.

1.

2.

The frogs _____ on the log.

The frog _____ on the log.

C. Read each sentence. Circle the correct word.

3. Many frogs (is, are) green.

4. Some frogs (is, are) very big.

5. But that frog (is, are) little.

Pronouns

INTRODUCTION

Invite students to draw a picture of their favorite food. As volunteers display their drawings, use the sentence frame *(Name) likes to eat (food)*. Repeat the sentence using a pronoun in place of the name. Ask questions that guide students to understand how the sentence changed. Point out that pronouns can take the place of special nouns. Write pronouns on the board (*I, you, he, she, it, we, they*). Provide examples of each.

Beginning

Part A: Distribute page 87. Direct students to look at the picture of the girl and boy eating pizza. Read the sentences aloud and have students repeat them. Ask the following questions about the sentences:
• *What is the name of the girl? Point to it.*
• *Look at the second sentence. What word is in dark print? Point to it.*
• *Does the word* she *take the place of the name Jane?*

Tell students that *she* is a pronoun that takes the place of the name *Jane*. Remind them of the other pronouns on the board.

Part B: Tell students they will circle pronouns that name the people in pictures. Direct students to look at the picture of the boy. Ask questions that help students choose the correct pronoun. Repeat with the next picture.

Part C: Tell students they will write pronouns that take the place of special nouns. Read the words in the box. Then read aloud the first sentence. Ask students to repeat the underlined word or words. Ask questions about the sentence to help students choose the correct pronoun. Continue the process with the remaining sentences.

Intermediate

Part A: Follow the directions in Part A of the Beginning section, but substitute these questions:
• *What is the name of the girl?*
• *What word is in dark print in the second sentence?*
• *Does the word* she *take the place of the name Jane?*

Part B: Follow the directions in Part B of the Beginning section.

Part C: Tell students they will write pronouns that take the place of special nouns. Read the words in the box. Then read aloud the first sentence. Ask students to repeat the underlined word or words. Ask questions about the sentence to help students choose the correct pronoun. Read aloud the remaining sentences and pause to allow students to write their answers.

Advanced

Part A: Distribute page 87. Direct students to look at the picture of the girl and boy eating pizza. Read the sentences aloud and have students repeat them. Invite students to talk about the picture. Tell students that *she* is a pronoun that takes the place of the name *Jane*. Remind them of the other pronouns on the board.

Parts B and C: Read aloud the directions. Identify the pictures and read aloud the sentences. Have students complete the page independently.

EXTENSION

Say sentences about the students using their names. Challenge the students to repeat the sentences using pronouns. (*Lana wears a red shirt. Maria and Pablo have brown eyes.*)

Pronouns

A. Read the sentences.

Jane eats pizza.
She eats pizza.

B. Circle the word that matches the picture.

1.

he   it

2.

they   you

C. Write a word from the box that can take the place of the underlined word or words.

┌─────────────────────────┐
│ They   He   It │
└─────────────────────────┘

3. <u>Keno</u> got a pizza. _____

4. <u>The pizza</u> was very big. _____

5. <u>Jay and Lisa</u> help eat the pizza. _____

Describing Words

INTRODUCTION

Review color names and number words. Then, invite volunteers to describe the colors of their clothes and the number of each article. Explain to students that color and number words are describing words, or adjectives.

Beginning

Part A: Distribute page 89. Direct students to look at the picture of the girl and the snowman. Read the sentence aloud and have students repeat it. Ask the following questions about the picture:
• *Is the girl outside?*
• *Is the girl wearing a coat?*
• *Is snow cold?*

Tell students that *cold* is a describing word, or adjective. Explain that a describing word can tell about color, size, or shape. It can also tell about how something feels, tastes, sounds, or smells.

Part B: Tell students they will circle describing words that tell about a picture. Direct students to look at the picture of the boy. Ask questions that help students choose the correct adjective. Repeat with the next picture.

Part C: Tell students they will write describing words that complete sentences. Slowly read the describing words in the box as students point to them and repeat them. Then, identify the picture of the dog. Read the sentences and substitute each describing word. Ask questions about the picture and sentences to help students choose the correct adjective. Guide students to write *dirty* on the line and mark it out in the box. Continue the process with the remaining sentences.

Intermediate

Part A: Follow the directions in Part A of the Beginning section, but substitute these questions:
• *Is the girl inside or outside?*
• *Is the girl playing in water or snow?*
• *Is snow hot or cold?*

Part B: Follow the directions in Part B of the Beginning section.

Part C: Tell students they will write describing words that complete sentences. Slowly read the describing words in the box as students point to them and repeat them. Then, identify the picture of the dog. Read the sentences and substitute each describing word. Guide students to write *dirty* on the line and mark it out in the box. Read aloud the remaining sentences and pause to allow students to write their answers.

Advanced

Part A: Distribute page 89. Direct students to look at the picture of the girl and the snowman. Read the sentence aloud and have students repeat it. Invite students to talk about the picture. Tell students that *cold* is a describing word, or adjective. Explain that a describing word can tell about color, size, or shape. It can also tell about how something feels, tastes, sounds, or smells.

Parts B and C: Read aloud the directions. Identify the pictures and read aloud the words and sentences. Have students complete the page independently.

EXTENSION

Say sentences about the students using their names. Challenge the students to repeat the sentences using describing words. (*Lana wears a red shirt. Maria and Pablo have brown eyes.*)

Describing Words

A. Read the sentence.

It is **cold** outside.

B. Circle the word that matches the picture.

1.

happy   sad

2.

big   wet

C. Write a word from the box to complete the sentence.

hot   dirty   green

3.

Max plays in the mud. He is _____.

4.

Stay away from the fire. It is _____.

5.

Look at the frog. It is _____.

Compound Words

INTRODUCTION

Display a raincoat. Lead students in a discussion of when the coat is used. Write *raincoat* on the board. Say the word and have students repeat it. Explain that *raincoat* is a compound word and that compound words are made up of two smaller words joined together. Then write the following under the word: *rain + coat = raincoat*.

Beginning

Part A: Distribute page 91. Direct students to look at the picture of the students eating. Read the sentence aloud and have students repeat it. Ask the following questions about the sentence:
• *Are the students eating lunch?*
• *Are the students in a room?*

Have students point to the word *lunchroom* in the sentence. Explain that *lunchroom* is made of the two smaller words *lunch* and *room*. Remind students that a compound word is made of two smaller words joined together.

Part B: Tell students they will write the two smaller words in *lunchroom*. Direct students to look at the picture of the lunch tray. Ask questions that help students write *lunch*. Repeat with the picture of the room.

Part C: Tell students they will write compound words. Have students point to the picture of the girls on the playground. Ask questions that help students understand where the girls are. Then, slowly read the words beside the picture as students point to them and repeat them. Guide students to write *playground* on the line. Have them say the word. Continue the process with the remaining words.

Intermediate

Part A: Follow the directions in Part A of the Beginning section, but substitute these questions:
• *Are the students eating lunch or playing games?*
• *Are the students in a room or on the playground?*

Part B: Follow the directions in Part B of the Beginning section.

Part C: Tell students they will write compound words. Have students point to the picture of the girls on the playground. Ask questions that help students understand where the girls are. Then, slowly read the words beside the picture as students point to them and repeat them. Guide students to write *playground* on the line. Have them say the word. Ask questions about the remaining pictures and pause to allow students to write their answers. Have them say the compound words.

Advanced

Part A: Distribute page 91. Direct students to look at the picture of the students eating. Read the sentence aloud and have students repeat it. Invite students to talk about the picture. Have students point to the word *lunchroom*. Explain that *lunchroom* is made of the two smaller words *lunch* and *room*. Remind students that a compound word is made of two smaller words joined together.

Parts B and C: Read aloud the directions. Ask questions about the pictures. Have students complete the page independently.

E X T E N S I O N

Prepare a list of compound words. Write the first word of each compound in one column on the board and the second word in another column. Challenge students to draw lines to make compound words and then use them in sentences.

Compound Words

A. Read the sentence.

We eat in the **lunchroom**.

B. Write the two words in **lunchroom**.

1.

2.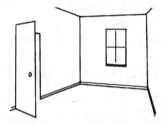

_____   _____

C. Write the words together to make each compound word.

3.

play + ground = _____

4.

birth + day = _____

5.

basket + ball = _____

Contractions

INTRODUCTION

Write *cannot* on the board and use the word in a sentence. Tell students that some words in the English language can be made shorter. Erase the *no* and add an apostrophe to make the contraction *can't*. Explain that the little mark that takes the place of the letters is an apostrophe. Repeat the initial sentence using the contraction *can't*.

Beginning

Part A: Distribute page 93. Direct students to look at the picture of the girl. Read the sentences aloud and have students repeat them. Ask the following questions about the sentences:

• *Look at the first sentence. Where are the words* does not*? Point to them.*
• *Look at the second sentence. What word is in dark print? Point to it.*
• *Does the word* doesn't *take the place of the words* does not*?*
• *Is the letter* n *or* o *missing in* doesn't*?*

Tell students that *doesn't* is a contraction that is a short form for the words *does not*. Remind them that the apostrophe, the little mark in the word, shows that a letter or letters are missing in a word.

Part B: Tell students they will draw lines to match pairs of words with their contractions. Read each pair of words and ask questions that help students find and draw lines to the corresponding contraction.

Part C: Tell students they will write contractions that make pairs of words shorter. Read the words in the box. Then, read aloud the first sentence. Ask students to repeat the underlined words. Ask questions about the sentence to help students choose the correct contraction. Have them say the word. Continue the process with the remaining sentences.

Intermediate

Part A: Follow the directions in Part A of the Beginning section, but substitute these questions:

• *Look at the words in dark print in the first sentence. Are the words* does not *or* cannot*?*
• *Look at the word in dark print in the second sentence. Is the word* doesn't *or* can't*?*
• *Does the word* doesn't *take the place of the words* does not*?*
• *What letters are missing in* doesn't*?*

Part B: Follow the directions in Part B of the Beginning section.

Part C: Tell students they will write contractions that make pairs of words shorter. Read the words in the box. Then, read aloud the first sentence. Ask students to repeat the underlined words. Ask questions about the sentence to help students choose the correct contraction. Have them write and say the word. Read aloud the remaining sentences and pause to allow students to write their answers.

Advanced

Part A: Distribute page 93. Direct students to look at the picture of the girl. Slowly read the sentences aloud and have students repeat them. Invite students to talk about the picture. Tell students that *doesn't* is a contraction that is a short form for the words *does not*. Remind them that the apostrophe, the little mark in the word, shows that a letter or letters are missing in a word.

Parts B and C: Read aloud the directions. Identify the words and read aloud the sentences. Have students complete the page independently.

EXTENSION

Say sentences that use pairs of words that can be made into contractions. Challenge students to repeat the sentences using contractions. (*I do not have a pencil. We should not talk loudly.*)

Contractions

A. Read the sentences.

The shirt **does not** fit.
The shirt **doesn't** fit.

B. Draw lines to match two words with the contraction.

1. is not   haven't

2. did not   isn't

3. have not   didn't

C. Write a word from the box that can take the place of the underlined word or words.

can't   don't   isn't

4. I <u>do not</u> like the shirt. _____

5. I <u>cannot</u> wear the shirt. _____

6. It <u>is not</u> my size. _____

Prefixes

INTRODUCTION

Invite a volunteer who is wearing a tennis shoe to untie it and take it off. Write *untie* on the board. Now, ask the volunteer to put the shoe on and retie it. Now write *retie* on the board. Ask students how the words are alike and different. Help them realize that the first two letters are different. Explain that small word parts, called prefixes, can be added to the beginning of some words to change their meaning. Tell students that the word part *un* means "not," so *untie* means "not tie." Continue to explain that *re* means "again," so *retie* means "to tie again."

Beginning

Part A: Distribute page 95. Direct students to look at the picture of the boy. Read the sentences aloud and have students repeat them. Ask the following questions about the sentences:
• *This boy is not happy. How can you tell this? Point to it.*
• *What word in dark print means "not happy"? Point to it.*
• *Is the boy building the fence again?*
• *What word in dark print means "to build again"? Point to it.*

Tell students that *unhappy* means "not happy," and *rebuild* means "to build again." Remind them that the small word parts *re* and *un* are prefixes.

Part B: Tell students they will write words that match some definitions. Read each definition and ask questions that help students find and write the corresponding word with a prefix from Part A.

Part C: Tell students they will write words that have prefixes to complete sentences. Slowly read the words in the box as students point to them and repeat them. Then, read the first sentence and substitute each word with a prefix. Ask questions about the sentence to help students choose the correct word. Guide students to write *unpack* on the line and mark it out in the box. Continue the process with the remaining sentences.

Intermediate

Part A: Follow the directions in Part A of the Beginning section, but substitute these questions:
• *What word in dark print means "not happy"?*
• *What word in dark print means "to build again"?*

Part B: Follow the directions in Part B of the Beginning section.

Part C: Tell students they will write words that have prefixes to complete sentences. Slowly read the words in the box as students point to them and repeat them. Then, read the first sentence and substitute each word with a prefix. Ask questions about the sentence to help students choose the correct word. Guide students to write *unpack* on the line and mark it out in the box. Read aloud the remaining sentences and pause to allow students to write their answers.

Advanced

Part A: Distribute page 95. Direct students to look at the picture of the boy. Read the sentences aloud and have students repeat them. Invite students to talk about the picture. Tell students that *unhappy* means "not happy," and *rebuild* means "to build again." Remind them that the small word parts *re* and *un* are prefixes.

Parts B and C: Read aloud the directions. Identify the words and read aloud the sentences. Have students complete the page independently.

EXTENSION

Introduce the word *recycle* and discuss its meaning. Ask students to tell examples of ways they recycle.

Prefixes

A. Read the sentences.

Tim was **unhappy**.
He had to **rebuild** the fence.

B. Write a word that matches each meaning. Use the words in dark print above.

1. to build again _____

2. not happy _____

C. Write a word from the box to complete the sentence.

repaint	reread	unlock	unpack

3. We will _____ the bag.

4. Jan needs to _____ the wall.

5. Use the key to _____ the door.

6. Hua wants to _____ the book.

Suffixes

INTRODUCTION

Write *thankful* on the board. Explain the meaning and ask students what they are thankful for. Next, write *quietly* on the board and have students tell where they must talk quietly. Then, underline the suffixes in each word. Point out that small word parts, called suffixes, can be added to the end of some words to change their meaning. Tell students that the word part *ful* means "full of," so *thankful* means "full of thanks." Continue to explain that *ly* means "done in a certain way," so *quietly* means "done quietly."

Beginning

Part A: Distribute page 97. Direct students to look at the picture of the dog. Read the sentences aloud and have students repeat them. Ask the following questions about the sentences:
• *Is this dog playing?*
• *What word in dark print means "full of play"? Point to it.*
• *Is the dog moving in a way that is quick?*
• *What word in dark print means "in a quick way"? Point to it.*

Tell students that *playful* means "full of play," and *quickly* means "in a quick way." Remind them that the small word parts *ful* and *ly* are suffixes.

Part B: Tell students they will write words that match some definitions. Read each definition and ask questions that help students find and write the corresponding word with a suffix from Part A.

Part C: Tell students they will write words that have suffixes to complete sentences. Slowly read the words in the box as students point to them and repeat them. Then, read the first sentence and substitute each word with a suffix. Ask questions about the sentence to help students choose the correct word. Guide students to write *loudly* on the

line and mark it out in the box. Continue the process with the remaining sentences.

Intermediate

Part A: Follow the directions in Part A of the Beginning section, but substitute these questions:
• *What word in dark print means "full of play"?*
• *What word in dark print means "in a quick way"?*

Part B: Follow the directions in Part B of the Beginning section.

Part C: Tell students they will write words that have suffixes to complete sentences. Slowly read the words in the box as students point to them and repeat them. Then, read the first sentence and substitute each word with a suffix. Ask questions about the sentence to help students choose the correct word. Guide students to write *loudly* on the line and mark it out in the box. Read aloud the remaining sentences and pause to allow students to write their answers.

Advanced

Part A: Distribute page 97. Direct students to look at the picture of the dog. Read the sentences aloud and have students repeat them. Invite students to talk about the picture. Tell students that *playful* means "full of play," and *quickly* means "in a quick way." Remind them that the small word parts *ful* and *ly* are suffixes.

Parts B and C: Read aloud the directions. Identify the words and read aloud the sentences. Have students complete the page independently.

EXTENSION

Invite volunteers to demonstrate movements for the following words: *slowly, quickly, softly,* and *loudly.*

Name _____   Date _____

Suffixes

A. Read the sentences.

Ben was **playful**.
He chased his tail **quickly**.

B. Write a word that matches each meaning. Use the words in dark print above.

1. full of play _____

2. in a quick way _____

C. Write a word from the box to complete the sentence.

helpful	harmful	slowly	loudly

3. The people yelled _____ during the game.

4. Sweets are _____ to the teeth.

5. Jim was _____ when he washed the dishes.

6. A turtle walks _____.

Body Parts

INTRODUCTION

Teach students the song and movements to the song "Head, Shoulders, Knees, and Toes." Invite students to name other body parts they know in English. Explain that all of the parts together make up the body.

 Invite students to share the sequence of words for the song above in their native language.

Beginning

Part A: Distribute page 99. Direct students to look at the picture of the children dancing. Read the sentence aloud and have students repeat it. Ask the following questions about the sentence:
• *Are the children dancing?*
• *What parts of their bodies are moving? Show me by pointing to those parts on yourself.*

As students point to each body part, identify the part and have them repeat the name. Remind them that all these parts make up the body.

Part B: Tell students they will write words to identify the parts of the body. Slowly read the first word in the box. Have students point to the word and repeat it. Ask questions that help students find that part on themselves. Then, have them find the same part on the figure and write it on the line. Continue the process with each word.

Intermediate

Part A: Follow the directions in Part A of the Beginning section, but substitute these questions:
• *Are the children dancing or running?*
• *What body parts are moving?*

Part B: Tell students they will write words to identify the parts of the body. Slowly read each word in the box. Have students point to the word and repeat it. Ask questions that help students point to that part on themselves. Have students work with a partner to complete the page.

Advanced

Part A: Distribute page 99. Direct students to look at the picture of the children dancing. Read the sentence aloud and have students repeat it. Invite students to talk about the picture. As students point to each body part, identify the part and have them repeat the name. Remind them that all these parts make up the body.

Part B: Read aloud the directions and the words in the box. Have students complete the page independently.

EXTENSION

Invite students to make life-sized paper cutouts by lying down on butcher paper and having a partner trace the body. Help students label the different body parts. Save the outline for the extension activity for the lesson on clothing.

Name _____   Date _____

Body Parts

A. Read the sentence.

The **body** can move in many ways.

B. Write the word that matches the body part.

eye	toe	arm	hand	foot	mouth
ear	leg	head	knee	nose	shoulder

Clothing

INTRODUCTION

Gather two sets each of the following articles of large-sized clothing: shirt, pants, socks, and shoes. Identify each article. Then, place each set in a separate box having students repeat the names as you put each piece in the box. Next, assign the students to two teams and invite them to participate in a relay. One person from each team puts on all the clothes. They run to a set place and back to their team, where they remove the clothing. The next player repeats the process. The first team to have all players complete the course wins.

 Invite students to share the names of the above clothing in their native language.

Beginning

Part A: Distribute page 101. Direct students to look at the picture of the clothes. Read the sentence aloud and have students repeat it. Then, have students point to each piece of clothing on the clothesline as you say the name. Have them repeat the names. Ask the following questions about the sentence:
- *The word in dark print is* clothes. *Do you see clothes on the line?*
- *Where are the pants? socks? shoes? Show me.*
- *Where is the shirt? skirt? dress? hat? coat? Show me.*

Next, say the names of clothing and have students point to the ones they are wearing. If other clothing is being worn, identify it and have students repeat the word. Remind them that all these words name kinds of clothes.

Part B: Tell students that the names of clothing are all mixed up. Explain that they need to write the words correctly and then draw that piece clothing. Invite a volunteer to call out the letters of a word as you write them on the board. Model how to search the list in Part A for the word. Write the word correctly and have students point to that article in Part A. Then, have them say the word. Allow them time to draw the item. Continue the process with each word.

Intermediate

Part A: Follow the directions in Part A of the Beginning section, but substitute these questions:
- *What is on the line?*
- *What clothes do you see?*

Part B: Tell students that the names of clothing are all mixed up. Explain that they need to write the words correctly and then draw that piece clothing. Invite a volunteer to call out the letters of a word as you write them on the board. Model how to search the list in Part A for the word. Write the word correctly and have students read it. Have students work with a partner to complete the page.

Advanced

Part A: Distribute page 101. Direct students to look at the picture of the clothes. Read the sentence aloud and have students repeat it. Invite students to talk about the picture. Next, say the names of clothing and have students raise their hands if they are wearing that kind of clothing. If other clothing is being worn, identify it and have students repeat the word. Remind them that all these words name kinds of clothes.

Part B: Read aloud the directions. Have students complete the page independently.

EXTENSION

Refer to the Extension activity in the lesson on body parts. Invite students to use art supplies to make clothes for their paper cutouts. Help students label the different kinds of clothing.

Clothing

A. Read the sentence.

shirt   pants   socks   coat   dress   hat   shoes   skirt

The **clothes** dry on the line.

B. The letters are mixed up. Write the names of clothes. Then draw a picture of each.

1. tha _____	**2.** taoc _____
3. triks _____	**4.** sresd _____
5. stanp _____	**6.** seohs _____
7. thirs _____	**8.** skocs _____

Colors

INTRODUCTION

As you hold up each crayon, sing a revised version of the song "Skip to My Lou." You may wish to sing the first sentence in each line and have children echo it.

A rose is red, a rose is red.
A rose is red, a rose is red.
A rose is red, a rose is red.
Find this crayon and show me!

Repeat with these color sentences: *A fish is orange; The sun is yellow; The grass is green; The sea is blue; The grapes are purple; The snow is white; A crow is black.*

 Invite students to share color words in their native language.

 The homograph *color* may confuse students. Explain that *color* has two meanings. Pantomime the action of coloring and then hold up crayons, naming colors. Say simple sentences using the word in both ways and encourage students to pantomime the action or point to a crayon to show the way the word is used.

Beginning

Part A: Distribute page 103. Direct students to look at the picture of the crayons. Read the sentence aloud and have students repeat it. Then, hold up crayons in the order shown on the page. Say each name and have students repeat it. Then, have students point to the color word on the page and color the crayon to match. Ask the following questions about the sentence:
• *What is a crayon? Show me.*
• *What color is red? blue? orange? white? Show me.*

Next, invite students to sing the song as they hold up the corresponding crayon.

Part B: Tell students that they will color the pictures to match the things in the song. Say each picture name and have students point to it and repeat the name. Then, invite students to sing the first verse of the song as they look for that color crayon. Have them color the rose. Continue the process with each color.

Intermediate

Part A: Follow the directions in Part A of the Beginning section, but substitute these questions:
• *What come in many colors?*
• *What colors do you see? Hold up the crayon as you say the color word.*

Part B: Tell students that they will color the pictures to match the things in the song. Say each picture name and have students point to it and repeat the name. Then, invite students to sing all the verses of the color song. Have students work with a partner to color the items to match ones in the song.

Advanced

Part A: Distribute page 103. Direct students to look at the picture of the crayons. Read the sentence aloud and have students repeat it. Invite students to talk about the color names they see. Next, say the colors and have students raise their hands if they are wearing clothing with that color. Have them color the crayons to match the colors.

Part B: Read aloud the directions. Repeat the song if necessary. Then, have students complete the page independently.

EXTENSION

Invite students to go on a color scavenger hunt. Assign pairs of students a color. Have them gather items with that color. If possible, award a small prize to the pair that finds the most items.

Colors

A. Read the sentence.

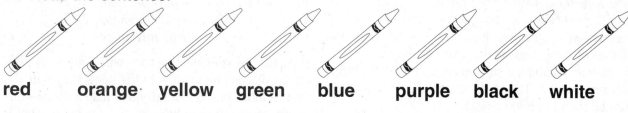

red   **orange**   **yellow**   **green**   **blue**   **purple**   **black**   **white**

Crayons come in many **colors**.

B. Color each item so it matches the one named in the color song.

Places in a Community

INTRODUCTION

Gather items that represent places in a community, like a stamped letter to symbolize the post office and something with a price tag to symbolize a store. Hold each item up and lead students in a discussion of where each could be found. Write the names of the places on the board as they are identified. Challenge students to name other places not represented. Tell students that all of the places can be found in a town or city.

 Invite students to tell about special place words in their native language.

Beginning

Part A: Distribute page 105. Direct students to look at the picture of the street scene. Read the sentence aloud and have students repeat it. Invite groups of students to role-play shopping and playing. Ask the following questions about the sentence:
• *Can you find a place to shop in this town? Point to it.*
• *Can you find a place to play in this town? Point to it.*
• *Which word in the sentence is* town*? Point to it.*

Part B: Tell students that they will draw lines to match places in a town with the items they will find in those places. Say *library* and have students place their finger on that picture and repeat the name. Lead children in a discussion of what a library is. Guide them to find the books in the second column and draw a line between the two. Continue the process with each place.

Intermediate

Part A: Follow the directions in Part A of the Beginning section, but substitute these questions:
• *Is a store a place to play or shop?*
• *Is a park a place to play or shop?*
• *What place does the picture show?*

Part B: Tell students that they will draw lines to match places in a town with the items they will find in those places. Identify and lead a discussion about each picture to be sure students know what is shown. Then, encourage them to repeat the picture names. Have students work with a partner to complete the page.

Advanced

Part A: Distribute page 105. Direct students to look at the picture of the street scene. Read the sentence aloud and have students repeat it. Invite students to talk about the picture. Challenge students to name stores they know about like the ones shown in the picture. Remind students that these places can be found in most towns.

Part B: Read aloud the directions. Identify the pictures and discuss the ones students are unfamiliar with. Then, have students complete the page independently.

EXTENSION

Invite students to draw a picture of a place in their town they like to visit. Help them write a sentence telling why they like that place.

Name _____   Date _____

Places in a Community

A. Read the sentence.

A **town** has places to shop and play.

B. Draw lines to match the place with items you find there.

1.

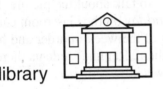

library

2.

post office

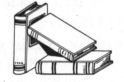

3.

park

4.

school

5.

store

Days of the Week

INTRODUCTION

Display a classroom calendar and point out the days of the week. Teach students this revised version of the song "Frère Jacques":

Sunday, Monday, Tuesday, Wednesday,
Are some days of the week.
Followed by Thursday, Friday, and Saturday.
Seven days make a week!

 Invite students to say the names of the days of the week in their native language.

Beginning

Part A: Distribute page 107. Direct students to look at the picture of the children playing soccer. Read the sentence aloud and have students repeat it. Invite students to tell about times they played soccer. Ask the following questions about the sentence:
• *Are these children in school?*
• *Are they playing soccer?*
• *Which word in the sentence is* Saturday*?*
  Point to it.

Have students find *Saturday* on the classroom calendar. Review the days of the week in order and have students repeat them.

Part B: Tell students that they will answer questions about the days of the week. Point out that the calendar will help them remember the order. Read each day on the calendar as students point to it and repeat it. Then, read aloud each question. Guide students to find the answer using the calendar and write the day on the line. Continue the process with each question.

Intermediate

Part A: Follow the directions in Part A of the Beginning section, but substitute these questions:
• *What game are the children playing?*
• *On what day are the children playing?*

Part B: Tell students that they will answer questions about the days of the week. Point out that the calendar will help them remember the order. Review the days of the week. Then, read aloud each question. Pause between each question so that students can write their answers.

Advanced

Part A: Distribute page 107. Direct students to look at the picture of the children playing soccer. Read the sentence aloud and have students repeat it. Invite students to talk about the picture. Have students find *Saturday* on the classroom calendar. Review the days of the week in order and have students repeat them. Remind students there are seven days in a week.

Part B: Read aloud the directions. Point out that the calendar will help students answer the questions. If necessary, read aloud the questions. Then, have students complete the page independently.

EXTENSION

Together, create a weekly calendar that shows the activities the class attends, such as a weekly library visit.

Name _____   Date _____

Days of the Week

A. Read the sentence.

Anne plays soccer on **Saturday**.

B. Use the calendar to answer the questions.

Sunday	Monday	Tuesday	Wednesday	Thursday	Friday	Saturday

1. What day comes after Tuesday? _____

2. What day comes before Friday? _____

3. What day comes after Sunday? _____

4. What two days start with the letter **S**? _____

_____

5. What days do you come to school? _____

_____

_____

_____

_____

Food

INTRODUCTION

Gather a food pyramid and example foods from each group. Display the pyramid and explain the categories. Next, name each food and have students repeat the names. Invite volunteers to tell in which category the food belongs on the food pyramid.

 Invite students to tell about a food they like from their native country and identify the food group to which it belongs.

Beginning

Part A: Distribute page 109. Direct students to look at the picture of the children in the lunchroom. Read the sentence aloud and have students repeat it. Invite students to tell about foods they like to eat. Ask the following questions about the picture and sentence:
• *What kinds of foods do you see in the picture? Point to them.*
• *Are the children in a lunchroom?*
• *Which word in the sentence is* food*? Point to it.*

Review the groups on the food pyramid.

Part B: Tell students that they will sort foods into the groups shown on the food pyramid. Say each picture name. Have students point to them and repeat the names. Then, have students cut apart the pictures. Ask questions that help students sort each food.

Intermediate

Part A: Follow the directions in Part A of the Beginning section, but substitute these questions:
• *Where are the children?*
• *What can they get in the lunchroom?*

Part B: Tell students that they will sort foods into the groups shown on the food pyramid. Say each picture name. Have students point to them and repeat the names. Then, have students cut apart the pictures and work with a partner to sort the pictures.

Advanced

Part A: Distribute page 109. Direct students to look at the picture of the children in the lunchroom. Read the sentence aloud and have students repeat it. Invite students to tell about foods they like to eat. Invite students to talk about the picture. Review the groups on the food pyramid.

Part B: Read aloud the directions. Identify the picture names. Then, have students sort the pictures independently.

EXTENSION

Create a large food pyramid on butcher paper. Invite students to look through recycled magazines and catalogues to cut out pictures to glue in the appropriate food category.

Food

A. Read the sentence.

Dan eats **food** that is good for him.

B. Cut out the pictures. Sort them into food pyramid groups.

© Steck-Vaughn Company

109

Unit 4: Vocabulary
ESL 2-3, SV 7097-1

Money

INTRODUCTION

Provide a handful of coins and invite students to sort them. Afterwards, name the coins, tell their value, and have students look at both sides of the coins. Tell students that the coins are some examples of American money. Encourage students to tell about experiences they have had buying things.

 Invite students to bring to class several coins from their native country.

Beginning

Part A: Distribute page 111. Direct students to look at the coins. Read the sentence aloud and have students repeat it. Review the coins, their values, and word names. Explain that there are several kinds of American money, but the ones they will learn now are coins. Ask the following questions about the sentence and pictures:
• *Which coin is the penny? nickel? dime? quarter? Point to it.*
• *Which word in the sentence is money? Point to it.*

Part B: Tell students that they will count groups of coins to find their amounts. Identify each coin in the first group and tell its value as students point to them and repeat the names. Then model how to count the coins by adding on. Repeat the pattern and have students write the amounts. Continue the process with each group of coins.

Intermediate

Part A: Follow the directions in Part A of the Beginning section.

Part B: Tell students that they will count groups of coins to find their amounts. Invite a volunteer to name the coins and their values in the first group. Then, model how to count the coins by adding on. Pause at the last coin for students to say the final value. Repeat with the remaining groups of coins.

Advanced

Part A: Distribute page 111. Direct students to look at the coins. Read the sentence aloud and have students repeat it. Review the coins, their values, and word names. Explain there are several kinds of American money, but the ones they will learn now are coins.

Part B: Read aloud the directions. Model how to count the first group of coins. Then, have students complete the page independently.

EXTENSION

Write price tags for small items, such as pencils and pens. Have students count out the coins needed to purchase the items.

Name _____   Date _____

Money

A. Read the sentence.

1 cent   5 cents   10 cents   25 cents

1¢   5¢   10¢   25¢

Money can buy things.

B. Count on to find the total amount.

1.

_____¢ _____¢ _____¢ _____¢ _____¢

2.

_____¢ _____¢ _____¢ _____¢

3.

_____¢ _____¢ _____¢ _____¢

4.

_____¢ _____¢ _____¢ _____¢ _____¢

School Tools

INTRODUCTION

Gather two sets of the following school items: pencil, pen, crayon, and chalk. Place one set in a bag. Hold up the chalk and say the name. Have students repeat it. Invite a volunteer to put their hand in the bag and find the chalk without looking. Have all the students say *chalk* when it is pulled out. Repeat with the other items.

 Invite students to name the school tools in their native language.

 The homograph *pen* may confuse students. Explain that *pen* has two meanings. It can be a name for a school tool or it can be the place where an animal lives. Say simple sentences using the word in both ways and encourage students to raise a hand when the word is used as a school tool.

Beginning

Part A: Distribute page 113. Direct students to look at the boy doing schoolwork. Read the sentence aloud and have students repeat it. Ask the following questions about the sentence and pictures:.
• *Is the boy cutting with scissors? Point to the scissors.*
• *Could the boy color with crayons? Point to the crayons.*
• *Could the boy write with a pencil? Point to the pencil.*
• *Which words in the sentence are* school tools? *Point to them.*

Point out that tools are things that help a person do work and school tools help them do schoolwork.

Part B: Tell students that they will cut out cards and play a game to match words. Have students point to the picture of the pencil. Say *pencil* and have students repeat it. Then, invite a volunteer to spell the word. Challenge students to find another card that has *pencil* on it. Continue the process with each school tool. Then, have students cut apart the cards and play Concentration with a partner.

Intermediate

Part A: Follow the directions in Part A of the Beginning section, but substitute these questions:
• *Is the boy cutting with scissors or a ruler?*
• *What can the boy write with?*

Part B: Tell students that they will cut out cards and play a game to match words. Have students point to the picture of the pencil. Say *pencil* and have students repeat it. Then, invite a volunteer to spell the word. Challenge students to find another card that has *pencil* on it. Identify the names of the remaining pictures as students point to them and repeat the names. Then, have students cut apart the cards and play Concentration with a partner.

Advanced

Part A: Distribute page 113. Direct students to look at the boy doing schoolwork. Read the sentence aloud and have students repeat it. Invite students to talk about the picture. Have them name the items on the desk and how they are used. Point out that tools are things that help a person do work and school tools help them do schoolwork.

Part B: Read aloud the directions. Invite volunteers to identify the tools and spell the words. Then, have partners play Concentration.

EXTENSION

Give each student two cards. Have them draw a picture of another school tool not named in the lesson. Help them write the name of the tool under the picture and write the name on the second card. Then, invite students to show their cards. Collect the cards and place them in a game center for students to play Concentration during their free time.

Name _____   Date _____

School Tools

A. Read the sentence.

We need **school tools** to do our work.

B. Cut out the cards. Find the two cards that go together.

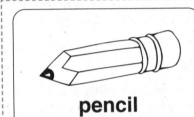 **pencil**	**pen**	**ruler**
 **scissors**	 **crayon**	 **glue**
glue	**pencil**	**ruler**
pen	**scissors**	**crayon**

Shapes

INTRODUCTION

Distribute shape blocks and challenge students to make a simple ABAB pattern. Help students name the shapes in their patterns.

 Invite students to identify the pattern using their native language.

Beginning

Part A: Distribute page 115. Direct students to look at the picture frames. Read the sentence aloud and have students repeat it. Say each shape name as students point to that frame and repeat the name. Ask the following questions about the sentence and picture:

• *Which frame looks like a square? rectangle? circle? triangle? Point to it.*

• *Which word in the sentence is* shapes*? Point to it.*

Remind students that a square, rectangle, circle, and triangle are all shapes.

Part B: Tell students that they will count shapes and write the number in a chart. Point out the chart and how to use it. Have students point to the circle in the chart. Model how to find and count circles in the bird and record the answer. Then, have students point to the square. Ask questions that help them count the squares in the bird and record the answer. Continue the process with the remaining shapes.

Intermediate

Part A: Follow the directions in Part A of the Beginning section.

Part B: Tell students that they will count shapes and write the number in a chart. Point out the chart and how to use it. Have students point to the circle in the chart. Model how to find and count circles in the bird and record the answer. Identify the remaining shapes. Have students work with a partner to complete the chart.

Advanced

Part A: Distribute page 115. Direct students to look at the picture frames. Read the sentence aloud and have students repeat it. Invite students to discuss the picture and name the shapes they see.

Part B: Read aloud the directions. Model how to count the circles and record the answer in the chart. Then, have students complete the page independently.

EXTENSION

Invite students to make pictures using shape blocks. Have partners work together to create a chart showing the total number of each shape.

Name _____ Date _____

Shapes

A. Read the sentence.

Pictures can have different **shapes**.

B. How many of each shape do you see? Complete the table.

Shape	◯	☐	▭	△
Number				

Signs

INTRODUCTION

Take students on a tour of the school to notice signs. Include EXIT signs, as well as room signs. Have them say the sign names as well as write or draw the signs they see. After the tour, discuss the signs the students have seen and the importance of signs.

 Invite students to draw a stop sign they might see in their native country.

Beginning

Part A: Distribute page 117. Direct students to look at the picture. Read the sentence aloud and have students repeat it. Guide students to look at the street sign and identify its meaning. Ask the following questions about the sentence and picture:
• *Does the sign tell people to walk?*
• *Does the sign tell people to stop walking?*
• *Which word in the sentence is* signs? *Point to it.*

Lead students in a discussion of why it is important to obey signs. Conclude by reminding students that following the information on signs keeps people safe.

Part B: Tell students that they will write the meanings of signs. Read aloud the words in the box as students point to them and repeat them. Then, have students point to the sign that means *danger*. Ask questions that help students find the word *danger*, write it on the line, and cross it out in the box. Continue the process with the remaining signs.

Intermediate

Part A: Follow the directions in Part A of the Beginning section, but substitute these questions:
• *Does the sign tell people to walk or not to walk?*
• *What does the word in bold print in the sentence say?*

Part B: Tell students that they will write the meanings of signs. Read aloud the words in the box as students point to them and repeat them. Then, have students point to the sign that means *danger*. Ask questions that help students find the word *danger*, write it on the line, and cross it out in the box. Identify the remaining signs and pause for students to find and write each answer.

Advanced

Part A: Distribute page 117. Direct students to look at the picture. Read the sentence aloud and have students repeat it. Invite students to discuss the picture and identify the meaning of the street sign. Lead students in a discussion of why it is important to obey signs. Conclude by reminding students that following the information on signs keeps people safe.

Part B: Read aloud the directions. Then, invite a volunteer to read the words in the box. Have students complete the page independently.

EXTENSION

Ask students to look around their neighborhood for other signs. Have them draw or write the words. Encourage students to share their signs with the class.

Name _____   Date _____

Signs

A. Read the sentence.

Street **signs** help people move safely.

B. Use words from the box. Write what each sign says.

| stop | danger | hospital | restaurant | don't walk | no bicycles |

1.

_____

2.

_____

3.

_____

4.

_____

5.

_____

6.

_____

Ways to Move

INTRODUCTION

Have students draw a picture on index cards of how they get to school. Use the cards to create a picture graph. Label the categories and have students repeat the category names. Ask questions about the groups to help them understand the data.

 Invite students to tell kinds of transportation they used in their native country.

Beginning

Part A: Distribute page 119. Direct students to look at the picture of the school. Read the sentence aloud and have students repeat it. Guide students to look at the school scene. Ask the following questions about the sentence and picture:
• *Is a child riding a bike to school? a bus? in a car? walking? Point to it.*
• *Which word in the sentence is* move*? Point to it.*

Explain to students that all the ways to move are kinds of transportation.

Part B: Tell students they will write words that name things that move. Identify the picture of the airplane as students point to it and repeat the word. Tell students that *airplane* is spelled *a, i, r, p, l, a, n, e.* Help them find the word in the list, write it on the line, and cross out the word in the box. Continue the process with the remaining pictures by identifying the picture and the spelling of the name.

Intermediate

Part A: Follow the directions in Part A of the Beginning section, but substitute these questions:
• *How are children getting to school?*
• *What does the word in bold print in the sentence say?*

Part B: Tell students they will write words that name things that move. Identify the picture of the airplane as students point to it and repeat the word. Tell students that *airplane* is spelled *a, i, r, p, l, a, n, e.* Help them find the word in the list, write it on the line, and cross out the word in the box. Help students identify the names of the remaining pictures and read the words. Ask students to work with a partner to complete the page.

Advanced

Part A: Distribute page 119. Direct students to look at the picture of the school. Read the sentence aloud and have students repeat it. Invite students to discuss the picture. Explain to students that all the ways to move are kinds of transportation.

Part B: Read aloud the directions. Then, invite a volunteer to read the words in the box and identify the pictures. Have students complete the page independently.

EXTENSION

Ask students to think of other kinds of transportation they have seen or used. Have them make a class mural showing all the different kinds of transportation and label each kind.

Name _____   Date _____

Ways to Move

A. Read the sentence.

There are many ways to **move** from place to place.

B. Write the word that names the picture.

| car   bus   bike   ship   truck   airplane |

1.

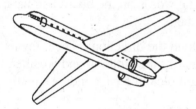

_____

2.

_____

3.

_____

4.

_____

5.

_____

6.

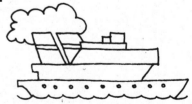

_____

Weather

INTRODUCTION

Invite students to draw a picture to show the day's weather. As students share their pictures, help them identify the words associated with the weather and write them on the board. Point to the words as you say them and have students repeat them.

 Invite students to tell what kind of weather is common in their native country.

Beginning

Part A: Distribute page 121. Direct students to look at the picture. Read the sentence aloud and have students repeat it. Ask the following questions about the sentence and picture:
• *Is it sunny in the picture?*
• *Is it raining in the picture?*
• *What kinds of things do people need if it rains?* Point to them.
• *Which word in the sentence is* weather? Point to it.

Invite students to name other kinds of weather. Write the words on the board and have students repeat them.

Part B: Tell students that they will draw lines to match the kinds of clothing people wear in different kinds of weather. Have students point to the jacket and mittens. Say the names and have students repeat them. Guide them to look at the pictures of the different kinds of weather. Identify each one. Ask questions that help students draw a line from the jacket to the snow scene. Continue the process with the remaining clothing.

Intermediate

Part A: Follow the directions in Part A of the Beginning section, but substitute these questions:
• *Is it sunny or rainy in the picture?*
• *Do people wear jackets or raincoats when it rains?*
• *What does the word in bold print in the sentence say?*

Part B: Tell students that they will draw lines to match the kinds of clothing people wear in different kinds of weather. Have students point to the jacket and mittens. Say the names and have students repeat them. Guide them to look at the pictures of the different kinds of weather. Identify each one as students point to them and repeat the names. Ask questions that help students draw a line from the jacket to the snow scene. Identify the remaining kinds of clothing. Have students work independently to complete the page.

Advanced

Part A: Distribute page 121. Direct students to look at the picture. Read the sentence aloud and have students repeat it. Invite students to discuss the picture. Invite students to name other kinds of weather. Write the words on the board and have students repeat them.

Part B: Read aloud the directions. Then, invite volunteers to identify the clothing and weather. Have students complete the page independently.

EXTENSION

Track the weather for one week. Discuss the changes the students noticed and how the weather affected their choice of clothing.

Weather

A. Read the sentence.

The **weather** is rainy today.

B. Draw lines to match the clothes with the weather.

1.

a.

2.

b.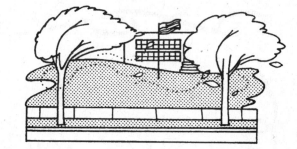

3.

c.

4.

d.

Dear _____,

You are doing a great job!
Keep up the good work.

_____

Great job, _____!

You know your

_____.

_____

The United States has other symbols, too.
The eagle is an important symbol.
The eagle is a large bird.
It is very strong, too.
Americans like to think they are strong like the eagle.

You can find the American flag at school.
You can also find one at the post office.
Many people fly a flag on July Fourth, too.
July Fourth is a special American holiday.
It is the day Americans said they would not follow English rule.
The flag shows that people are proud.

The Liberty Bell is another symbol of the United States.
It was made over two hundred years ago.
The bell has a big crack in it.
Long ago, Americans rang the bell when they wanted to tell important news.
Some news was good.
Some news was bad.

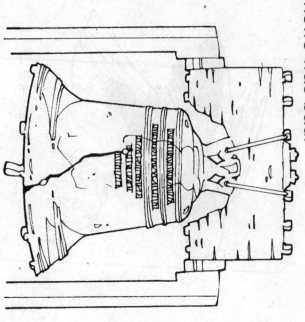

A symbol is something that has a special meaning.
The United States has some symbols.
The American flag is one very special symbol.
The American flag is red, white, and blue.
It has fifty white stars.
The stripes are red and white.

The Statue of Liberty is a symbol of freedom.
Long ago, many people left their countries.
They sailed across the ocean.
They came to live in the United States.
They wanted to be free and to have a better life.
The Statue of Liberty was the first thing they saw.
The statue became a special symbol for them, too.

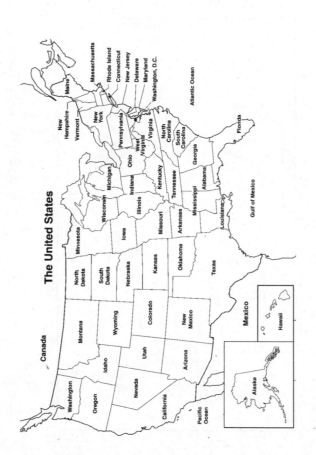

The United States is divided into states.
Some states have lots of mountains.
Some have hot deserts.
Other states are near the ocean.
Some states have a little of everything.
Can you find the state you live in?

The United States

American Symbols

The world is a big place.
It has large areas of land and water.
There are many countries, too.
The United States is one of those countries.
The United States also has another name.
It is called America.

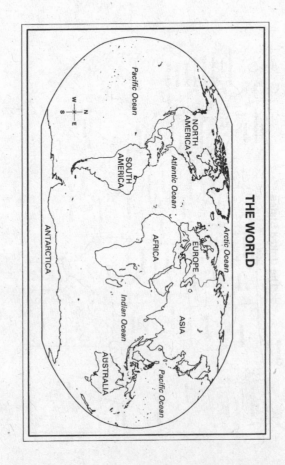

THE WORLD

Today, many people still come to the United States.
Just like long ago, they want to be free.
They want to have a better life.
It is hard work to learn the language.
It is hard to learn a new way of life.
But soon, these people will become Americans, too.
They will be proud of all American symbols.

3rd Grade — Pinewood School

ESL Grades 2–3

Answer Key

Page 5
Check that students follow the arrows to make circles and lines.

Page 6
Top shelf: picture of the ball and the word *top*.
Middle shelf: picture of the books and the word *middle*
Bottom shelf: picture of the car and the word *bottom*

Page 7
Check that students write the words in the correct places. Check that they glue the pictures of the cars on the left and the pictures of the bicycles on the right.

Page 8
1. bird or sun; above
2. sun or bird; above
3. fish or crab; below
4. crab or fish; below

Page 9
1. Students draw a bird under the cage.
2. Students draw a bird beside the cage.
3. Students draw a bird in the cage.
4. Students draw a bird on the cage.

Page 10
1. Students draw wheels on the second car.
2. Students draw windows on the second house.
3. Students draw a shirt with a heart on the second bear.

Page 11
1. Students write an X on the third table.
2. Students write an X on the first cat.
3. Students write an X on the second pizza.

Page 12
Students can sort the children into the following groups:
Children with balls; children with jump ropes.
Children wearing striped shirts; children wearing plain shirts.
Children wearing shorts; children wearing pants.
Children with dark hair; children with light hair.

Page 13
1. Order: first, next, last
2. Order: last, first, next
3. Order: last, next, first

Page 14
Check that students connect the dots from 0 to 10 to show both a barn and a wagon.

Page 15
Check that students write the correct number word name to match the numeral on the book spine.

Page 16
Check that students draw a line to the numerals in order from 1 to 20 through the maze.

Page 17
1. Check that students connect the dots of the capital letters of the alphabet to show a whale.
2. Check that students connect the dots of the lowercase letters of the alphabet to show a wagon.

Page 18
1. Students color Bb, Cc, Dd, and Ff.
2. Students color Gg, Hh, Jj, and Ll.
3. Students color Nn, Pp, Rr, and Ss.
4. Students color Uu, Vv, Ww, and Zz.

Page 19
1. b
2. v
3. h
4. f
5. l
6. s
7. p
8. t
9. w
10. z
11. r
12. k

Page 20
1. j
2. b
3. s
4. c
5. n
6. y
7. m
8. d
9. l
10. q
11. g
12. p

Page 21
Check students' work.

Page 22
Check students' work.

Page 23
Check students' work.

Page 24
1. listen
2. say
3. raise hand
4. look

Page 25
Check that students circle the butterfly, underline the bird, write their name on the tree, and color the sun.

Page 27
1. bat
2. cat
3. a
4. no letter
5. a
6. a
7. a
8. no letter

Page 29
1. bed
2. hen
3. bell
4. egg
5. web
6. desk
7. dress
8. pen

Page 31
1. pig
2. wig
3. pin
4. fish
5. ship
6. bib

Page 33
1. fox
2. box
3. o
4. o
5. no letter
6. no letter
7. o
8. o

Page 35
1. rug
2. bugs
3. tub
4. brush
5. bus
6. duck
7. drum
8. truck

Page 37
1. cape
2. ape
3. cane; picture of the cane
4. pane; picture of the window pane
5. cape; picture of the cape
6. tape; picture of the tape

Page 39
1. quail
2. hay
3. train
4. jay
5. tray
6. pail

Page 41
1. bee
2. leaf
3. feet
4. peas
5. eat
6. meat
7. sheep
8. queen

Page 43
1. ice
2. mice
3. kite
4. dime
5. bike
6. nine

Page 45
1. rose
2. mole
3. robe
4. hose
5. nose
6. rope
7. cone
8. home

Page 47
1. goat
2. coat
3. road
4. soap
5. toad
6. boat

Page 49
1. flute
2. mule
3. June
4. tube
5. tune
6. glue

Page 51
1. fly
2. puppy
3. happy
4. sky
5. bunny
6. cry

Page 53
1. star
2. car
3. jar
4. shark
5. arm
6. scarf
7. barn
8. yarn

Page 55
1. stork
2. corn
3. fork
4. horse
5. horn
6. porch

Page 57
1. fern
2. nurse
3. bird
4. herd
5. surf
6. girl
7. church
8. purse
9. shirt

Page 59
1. slide
2. swing
3. spoon
4. stamp
5. snake
6. skunk

Page 61
1. grapes
2. frog
3. tree
4. crab
5. brush
6. price

Page 63
1. gloves
2. plate
3. clown
4. flute
5. blocks
6. glue

Page 65
1. city
2. cat
3. fence
4. cut
5. pencil
6. face
7. can
8. cup

Page 67
1. garden
2. gerbil
3. giraffe
4. gum
5. goat
6. giant
7. dog
8. cage

Page 69
1. tissue
2. seal
3. nose
4. s
5. z
6. sh
7. sh
8. s
9. z

Page 71
1. children
2. whisper
3. ch
4. wh
5. wh
6. wh
7. ch
8. ch

Page 73
1. shirt
2. that
3. thirteen
4. sh
5. th
6. th
7. sh
8. th
9. sh

Page 75
1. boy
2. farm
3. goat
4. thing
5. person
6. place
7. person
8. place
9. thing

Page 77
1. Marco
2. South Street
3. Marco
4. Main Street
5. Stone Library
6. Emily

Page 79
1. log
2. frogs
3. books
4. brushes
5. trees

Page 81
1. waves
2. walks
3. sleeps
4. jump
5. swims

Page 83
1. climbed
2. pulled
3. visited
4. played
5. walked

Page 85
1. are
2. is
3. are
4. are
5. is

Page 87
1. he
2. they
3. He
4. It
5. They

Page 89
1. happy
2. big
3. dirty
4. hot
5. green

Page 91
1. lunch
2. room
3. playground
4. birthday
5. basketball

Page 93
1. isn't
2. didn't
3. haven't
4. don't
5. can't
6. isn't

Page 95
1. rebuild
2. unhappy
3. unpack
4. repaint
5. unlock
6. reread

Page 97
1. playful
2. quickly
3. loudly
4. harmful
5. helpful
6. slowly

Page 99
Check that students label the body parts correctly.

Page 101
1. hat
2. coat
3. skirt
4. dress
5. pants
6. shoes
7. shirt
8. socks

Page 103
Check students' coloring:
crow—black
grapes—purple
goldfish—orange
rose—red
grass—green
sun—yellow
ocean wave—blue
snowman—white

Page 105
1. books
2. stamp
3. swing
4. desk
5. food

Page 107
1. Wednesday
2. Thursday
3. Monday
4. Sunday and Saturday
5. Monday, Tuesday, Wednesday, Thursday, and Friday

Page 109
Breads, Cereal, Rice, Pasta: bread, cereal
Fruit: apple, grapes
Vegetables: peas, carrot
Meat, Poultry, Fish, Beans, Eggs, Nuts: meat, egg, fish
Milk, Yogurt, Cheese: milk, cheese
Fats, Oils, Sweets: cake

Page 111
1. 5
2. 16
3. 35
4. 75

Page 113
Check that students match the corresponding cards together.

Page 115
Circle: 2
Square: 4
Rectangle: 5
Triangle: 7

Page 117
1. danger
2. no bicycles
3. stop
4. restaurant
5. hospital
6. don't walk

Page 119
1. airplane
2. truck
3. car
4. bus
5. bike
6. ship

Page 121
1. c
2. a
3. d
4. b